THE TWILIGHT OF HUMAN RIGHTS LAW

Mark V. Tushnet
WILLIAM NELSON CROMWELL PROFESSOR OF
LAW
HARVARD LAW SCHOOL

J. Harvie Wilkinson
JUDGE
U.S. COURT OF APPEALS FOR THE FOURTH
CIRCUIT

GEOFFREY STONE AND OXFORD UNIVERSITY PRESS GRATEFULLY ACKNOWLEDGE THE INTEREST AND SUPPORT OF THE FOLLOWING ORGANIZATIONS IN THE INALIENABLE RIGHTS SERIES: THE ALA; THE CHICAGO HUMANITIES FESTIVAL; THE AMERICAN BAR ASSOCIATION; THE NATIONAL CONSTITUTION CENTER; THE NATIONAL ARCHIVES

The Twilight of Human Rights Law

Eric A. Posner

OXFORD
UNIVERSITY PRESS

OXFORD
UNIVERSITY PRESS

Oxford University Press is a department of the University of
Oxford. It furthers the University's objective of excellence in research,
scholarship, and education by publishing worldwide.

Oxford   New York
Auckland   Cape Town   Dar es Salaam   Hong Kong   Karachi
Kuala Lumpur   Madrid   Melbourne   Mexico City   Nairobi
New Delhi   Shanghai   Taipei   Toronto

With offices in
Argentina   Austria   Brazil   Chile   Czech Republic   France   Greece
Guatemala   Hungary   Italy   Japan   Poland   Portugal   Singapore
South Korea   Switzerland   Thailand   Turkey   Ukraine   Vietnam

Oxford is a registered trademark of Oxford University Press
in the UK and certain other countries.

Published in the United States of America by
Oxford University Press
198 Madison Avenue, New York, NY 10016

Library of Congress Cataloging-in-Publication Data
Posner, Eric A., author. The twilight of human rights law / Eric A. Posner.
p. cm.
ISBN 978-0-19-931344-0 (hardback : alk. paper)   1. Human rights.
2. Civil rights.   I. Title.
K3240.P69 2014
342.08'5—dc23

3 5 7 9 8 6 4
Printed in the United States of America
on acid-free paper

Contents

. . .

Editor's Note

. . .

> We hold these truths to be self-evident, that all men are created
> equal, that they are endowed by their Creator with certain
> unalienable Rights. . . .
>
> —The Declaration of Independence

Although the Inalienable Rights Series has thus far focused primarily on debate, deliberation, and discourse about American constitutional law, this volume reaches beyond the boundaries of the United States to explore the meaning of inalienable rights on the international stage. In this study of the origins, evolution, and enforcement of international human rights law, Eric Posner illuminates the relationship between the American conception of "inalienable rights" and the international conception of "human rights." To what extent are they similar? To what extent are they different? To the extent that they differ, why is this so? Should the United States look to expand its conception of inalienable rights to bring it more in line with the international understanding of human rights, or does the United States have a "better" notion of what rights should be thought to be truly fundamental?

Posner also explores how the substance of international human rights law has evolved over time, and how a broad range of international treaties, conventions, and institutions have attempted to give meaning to the concept of international human rights. These include, among many others, the Universal Declaration of Human Rights, the International Convention on the Elimination of All Forms of Racial Discrimination, the Convention Against Torture and Other Cruel, Inhuman or Degrading Treatment or Punishment, the Convention on the Rights of the Child, the Convention on the Elimination of All Forms of Discrimination Against Women, the Human Rights Committees, the UN Council on Human Rights, and the UN's Office of the High Commissioner for Human Rights.

Posner examines the extent to which nations actually comply with the principles of human rights law, the reasons why they comply, the reasons why they don't comply, and what, if anything, can be done to compel and encourage greater compliance. In the end, he concludes that, as currently constituted, international human rights law has little real impact. He thus calls for a more modest and more realistic approach that focuses more on effectiveness than on symbolism. *The Twilight of Human Rights Law* is thus an important, and no doubt provocative, cautionary tale about how trying to achieve too much can wind up achieving too little.

Geoffrey R. Stone
July 2014

THE TWILIGHT OF HUMAN RIGHTS LAW

Introduction

This is a good time for human rights. Not that they are respected more than in the past.[1]

—Joseph Raz

AMARILDO DE SOUZA, a bricklayer living in a favela in Rio de Janeiro, was arrested by police in an operation to round up drug traffickers in 2013. He was never seen again. When his wife complained, the police arrested her as well. De Souza's disappearance was taken up by protestors in street demonstrations, which in turn were also met with a ruthless police response. Normally, de Souza's story would have ended there, but public pressure led to a police investigation, and eventually the arrest of 10 police officers who have been charged with torturing and murdering him. Brazil's police are notoriously brutal; they are known to execute suspects and then claim that the suspects resisted arrest. Yet Brazil has an enormous amount of crime as well, and the police are given a free hand, including strong legal immunities. Every year more than a thousand killings by police—very likely executions, according to Human Rights Watch—take place in Rio de Janeiro alone.

When people think of the major human rights-violating countries, they think of places like North Korea, China, and Russia. Brazil, one of the largest democracies in the world, is rarely placed on that list, possibly because the Brazilian government—unlike the governments of North Korea, China, and Russia—does not harass or murder political dissenters. But the norm against extrajudicial killings is central to human rights law, and it is a norm that Brazil flagrantly violates—not as a matter of official policy, but as a matter of practice.

Brazil is hardly the only country where police combat crime, maintain order, or advance their own interests through extrajudicial killings. There are many such countries, including India, the world's largest democracy; the Philippines, where security forces routinely are involved in extrajudicial killings and disappearances; Malaysia, which has in recent years seen a rapid increase in the number of deaths of people in the custody of police; South Africa, where violent means are used against demonstrators as well as suspected criminals; Pakistan; Bangladesh; China; the Dominican Republic; Eritrea; Iran; and Sri Lanka. These countries, like Brazil, do not announce an official policy of extrajudicial killing. They all have court systems, and most suspected criminals are charged and appear in court. But the courts are slow and underfunded, so police, under pressure to combat crime, employ extrajudicial methods.

When police do use the court system, they often torture suspects in order to extract confessions, a practice that has been documented in many countries, including Greece, Lebanon, India, Mauritania, the United Arab Emirates, Ukraine, and Tajikistan. Torture is also commonly used by dictators to suppress political dissent—to intimidate political opponents, journalists, human rights workers, and others. Commonly cited examples include China, North Korea, Iraq,

States tortured suspected Al Qaeda
be dismissed as an aberration of the
ghtened country, but even before 9/11
d militants to Arab countries to be tor-
s in a process known as extraordinary
—including numerous liberal democ-
re—gave assistance to the U.S. effort
rogate, and detain suspected Islamic
rchers found that in 2011, torture was
countries (including Greece, Hungary,
65 countries (including France, Italy,
States), and not at all in 34 countries.[2]
rajudicial killings, and torture are fre-
ts in authoritarian states to suppress
ernments of such states employ a broad
heir power. In extreme cases, like China,
dependent political parties and refuses
countries that are effectively dictator-
ships or oligarchies include North Korea, Chad, Cuba, Syria, Saudi
Arabia, Uzbekistan, Ethiopia, Sudan, Libya, and Zimbabwe. Most
authoritarian governments keep power in subtler ways, maintaining
the formal mechanisms of democracy like elections, but controlling
them behind the scenes. In Russia, for example, the government
operates the major media outlets, censors other sources of news and
independent opinion, intimidates journalists, controls the judiciary
and uses it to conduct political trials of dissenters, and rigs elections. These practices also can be found in Cambodia, Afghanistan,
Venezuela, Haiti, Myanmar, the Democratic Republic of Congo,
Paraguay, Angola, Ukraine, and Yemen, among other countries. And,
of course, authoritarian countries also interfere with political associations, spy on citizens, and exploit popular prejudices by harassing
racial, ethnic, and sexual minorities.

Many of these countries also suppress or co-opt religious organizations for fear that they will become a source of opposition. China monitors religious organizations and punishes worshippers and clergy who belong to organizations, including Muslim and Catholic groups, that do not receive government approval. Religious persecution is especially common in Islamic countries, like Saudi Arabia, Pakistan, Afghanistan, and Sudan, where governments not only harass Christians and Jews but also Muslim sects that they regard as heretical.

Even age-old scourges like slavery continue to exist. A recent report estimates that nearly 30 million people are forced against their will to do work. Some of this slavery is the old-fashioned sort, where people are enslaved because of their ethnicity or caste. Modern human trafficking, where people are forced to travel to other countries to engage in forced labor like prostitution, is also included. The report estimates that about 14 million people are enslaved in India, nearly 3 million in China, more than 2 million in Pakistan, and hundreds of thousands in Nigeria, Ethiopia, Russia, Thailand, Congo, and Myanmar—the worst offenders.

In how many countries are human rights respected? This is a hard question to answer because many human rights are contested, and many human rights violations are not official policy but are tolerated or silently encouraged. One study by Freedom House counted 90 "free" countries out of 194 in 2013, where a free country is "one where there is open political competition, a climate of respect for civil liberties, significant independent civic life, and independent media."[3] The other countries experience a range of human rights abuses. The fraction of free countries in the world has gradually increased, from 29 percent in 1973, to 42 percent in 1991, to 46 percent in 2012.

Some commentators do not trust Freedom House because it is associated with conservative interests in the United States. Another study, relying on the Cingranelli-Richards Human Rights Dataset, which focuses on some common political rights plus workers' rights, tells roughly the same story: respect for rights has improved, but only modestly over the last 20 years—the period in which international human rights law finally became entrenched. But even countries that do well on these indices are not free of human rights abuses. Brazil and India are classified as "free" by Freedom House.

Countries that consistently receive the highest scores include the United States, Canada, Australia, New Zealand, and most European countries. These countries have democratic political systems and independent and competent judiciaries that protect people's rights. Yet they are also far from perfect from a human rights perspective. Human rights campaigners criticize the United States for its penal system, which incarcerates more people than does any other country; the death penalty; racial disparities in the criminal justice system; the treatment of noncitizens; and America's counterterrorism laws that permit indefinite detention and targeted killings on foreign battlefields. Some human rights organizations, including Human Rights Watch, also argue that the United States violates human rights by failing to provide more generous health and welfare benefits, protections for women and minorities, and support for labor unions.

Even the most humane and liberal European countries have violated the human rights of immigrants and other noncitizens. In some places, discrimination against the Roma is deeply entrenched and discrimination against Muslims is a significant problem. As noted above, a large number of European governments provided help to the CIA's program of detaining and torturing suspected members of al Qaeda in the years following the 9/11 attack. They also employ counterterrorism policies and general police practices (including preventive detention) that human rights advocates have criticized.

* * *

I started with the quotation from Joseph Raz, a distinguished legal philosopher, because it encapsulates a paradox about human rights. I will use the term *human rights discourse* to refer to the frequent invocation of human rights in public discussion, scholarly commentary, and government statements. Although people have always criticized their governments and foreign governments, they have not always done so in the distinctive idiom of human rights. They might say instead that *this* government has acted badly by breaking apart a political protest or *that* government has done poorly by failing to build an adequate school system. People who use the idiom of human rights instead argue that the first government violated rights to political participation and the second government violated rights to education. Raz is correct that human rights discourse is flourishing. And speakers do not simply assert that the rights exist; they point to a set of elaborate human rights treaties that incorporate those rights, treaties to which most governments have given their consent. Indeed, the use of "human rights" in English-speaking books has increased 200-fold since 1940, and is used today 100 times more than terms like "constitutional rights" and "natural rights."

And yet Raz is also roughly correct that human rights are not respected today more than in the past. I say "roughly correct" because of ambiguities in this statement. If the past means "the nineteenth century," then he is wrong: governments respect human rights more today than they did then. Most countries in the nineteenth century did not grant their citizens basic human rights like the right to vote. Those rights became increasingly common in the twentieth century, particularly after World War II, mainly in Western Europe, the United States, and a few other places. If he means the 1970s, then he is also wrong, but not tremendously wrong: human rights have improved since then, mainly thanks to the collapse of communism, but not much beyond that. But if he is referring to the last 20 years, he is correct that there has been little progress since the 1990s. What is odd about this pattern is that the advance of human rights as a *legal regime* began in the 1970s and accelerated in the 1980s—*before* countries agreed to international treaties that incorporate respect for human rights. This is puzzling.

The starting point for this book is that human rights law has failed to accomplish its objectives. More precisely, there is little evidence that human rights treaties, on the whole, have improved the well-being of people, or even resulted in respect for the rights in those treaties. The major goal of the book is to explain why. I address a number of possible or partial explanations, including some that are familiar—such as the relative weakness of the humanitarian impulses that lay behind human rights law and the ambiguity of the various strategic and instrumental bases for human rights. But my major argument is that human rights law reflects a kind of rule naiveté—the view that the good in every country can be reduced to a set of rules that can then be impartially enforced. Rule naiveté is in part responsible for the proliferation of human rights, which has made meaningful enforcement impossible.

In the last chapter of the book, I argue that if Westerners bear a moral responsibility to help less well-off people living in foreign countries, then they should start by learning the lessons of development economics. Animated by the same mix of altruism and concern for geopolitical stability as the human rights movement, development economics has also failed to achieve its mission, which is to promote economic growth. Yet its failures have led not to denial, but to experimentalism, incrementalism, and (increasingly) humility. Certain small-scale interventions can do good by relieving the worst forms of misery and poverty in the short term, and, as long as they are continuously subjected to rigorous empirical testing and found to be effective, they should be supported and continued.

Following this model, humanitarians should abandon the utopian aspirations of human rights law for the hard-won truths of development economics. It is time to wipe the slate clean and start over with an approach to promoting well-being in foreign countries that is empirical rather than ideological.

Although the book advances a specific argument about the efficacy and value of human rights law, I also intend it as a general introduction to the subject. You can learn about human rights law from this book even if you reject its argument. Chapters 1 and 2 provide an introductory survey of the history of human rights law, and the modern institutional embodiment of that law. Later chapters investigate the theoretical, empirical, and normative questions raised by the human rights regime. Chapters 3, 4, and 5 ask what is the best theoretical explanation for why states enter human rights treaties and comply with them (if they do), and examines the evidence. Chapter 6 discusses the relationship between human rights law and war. Chapter 7 discusses the normative questions. Throughout, I advance my argument that a human rights treaty regime can do little to improve the well-being of people around the world.

CHAPTER ONE

The History of International Human Rights Law

I.I. PREHISTORY—BEFORE WORLD WAR II

The animating idea behind human rights is the moral obligation not to harm strangers, and possibly the moral obligation to help them if they are in need. Most human groups—families, clans, tribes, nations, states—impose obligations on their members not to harm and, in most cases, to provide aid to, each other. These obligations are often strict, like the parents' obligation to care for their children, or the child's obligation to honor the parent. States may obligate citizens to fight and die for the sake of their co-nationals. These types of obligations stop at the border of the group. In Talmudic law, Jews may not lend at interest to other Jews, but may lend at interest to Gentiles. And, indeed, some groups do not forbid their members to harm strangers; it may be permissible to cheat, or rob, or even slaughter them. And even when constraints are imposed on the mistreatment of strangers, this is often pursuant to strategic imperatives, like the need to avoid war.

But there always coexisted with these basic moral structures a recognition of the common humanity of strangers, an acknowledgment that their well-being is entitled to consideration of some sort. In ancient literature, authors recognized people from other tribes or cultures as human beings, with similar wants and needs, and the capacity to suffer. The *Iliad* reaches its climax when Achilles permits King Priam to reclaim the corpse of his son, Hector, and give him proper burial rites. Perhaps some level of empathy for other human beings generally—not just members of the family or tribe or nation—is built into our biological makeup, or is learned by ordinary people as a matter of course. Tribes attack each other, but they also trade with each other, and intermarry, and these interactions would have made possible a sense that we owe obligations to others by virtue of their humanity (and so still excluding animals), even if those obligations are weaker than the obligations we owe to people in our family, tribe, or clan.

These ideas can be found in one form or another throughout recorded history, including in the major religions, and especially Christianity, with its radical notion that all humans are equal in the eyes of God. Anyone who harms another human being offends God; in this way, strangers may become an object of moral concern. Morality becomes universal in the sense that it applies to all human beings rather than to one's community or group alone.

Modern human rights thinking nonetheless did not develop until the Enlightenment in the eighteenth century. The historian Lynn Hunt argues that human rights evolved as a result of the expansion of literacy and reading, which exposed people to other human beings outside their immediate social, national, and kin groups, enabling them to learn that strangers are just like them.[1] This enhanced people's empathy for strangers and hence their receptiveness to the idea of human rights—that all human beings owe a moral obligation to all other human beings to respect their legitimate interests. Perhaps she is right, but the evidence that reading literature enhances people's capacity for empathy is weak.

A more plausible explanation for the development of theories of human rights in the Enlightenment is that Enlightenment thinkers believed that they needed to systematize moral thinking so as to defend themselves from the claim that secularization bred immorality. Seeking to throw off the influence of religion and irrational tradition, they needed to show that morality would persist in their absence, and they did so by locating the source of morality in human nature. If morality is a matter of human nature, then it is shared by all human beings.

It was a short step from there to the idea of human rights. Legal rights were well understood at the time. A legal right entitled a person to do something; if someone else tried to stop him, then the first person could seek aid from the government. Thus, a person who has an ownership right in land can seek aid from the government against trespassers and poachers. Enlightenment thinkers argued that just as people had rights against other people's interference with their property and lives, they also had rights against *government's* interference with their property and lives. What exactly these rights were and how one could vindicate them were complicated questions, but there was agreement that such rights existed, and that these rights were human rights. By virtue of a person's humanity, the government may not do certain things to him, like take his property without compensation, force him to quarter soldiers, or torture and kill him or his family.

The two major political documents that embodied these views were the U.S. Declaration of Independence, and the French Declaration of the Rights of Man. Both documents explained why the people could overthrow their government—because the government had violated their rights. (At the time, people often used the term "natural rights" rather than "human rights," but the terms meant the same thing.) The people could set up their own governments, and these governments would be required to comply with human rights.

But it was soon recognized that the political value of human rights was limited by a significant problem: the very idea that rights are universal conflicted with the imperative of building a nation. This is why human rights were a more powerful revolutionary idea than constitutional idea, mainly cited to explain why a government or foreign occupier was illegitimate, and not used to organize domestic constitutional arrangements. In the United States, human rights were domesticated as constitutional rights, which would for the most part protect Americans only, not foreigners (except those who came to settle in the United States). In France, human rights collapsed with Napoleon's dictatorship and the restoration of monarchy, after which, as in the United States, those rights took the form of constitutional protections for Frenchmen rather than universal imperatives applicable to all human beings.

Democratic impulses in Europe throughout the nineteenth century were closely allied with nationalism, which afforded the best hope for political organization on a large enough scale to provide for defense and domestic order. Great Britain provided a model. People possessed rights, but they were rights sanctified by history and tradition. Parliament respected the rights of Englishmen because of tradition, or because Englishmen demanded those rights, not because Englishmen are human beings. Other European countries that moved toward democracy or constitutional monarchy also recognized the rights of subjects or citizens because doing so brought political peace. The idea of human rights, that is, as rights enjoyed by all human beings irrespective of nationality, played a very small role, if any, in these developments.

This is not to say that people stopped taking an empathic interest in the well-being of foreigners. As I noted earlier, this seems like a basic stance of people, who are capable of feeling sympathy for "strangers" who are not a part of their community. People would thus feel distress when disasters struck foreigners, like the Lisbon earthquake of 1755. A deep popular revulsion toward slavery emerged in Great Britain in the nineteenth century, and it was revulsion toward slavery wherever it existed, anywhere in the world, rather than only slavery on British soil. Motivated by, or at least intertwined with, their religious convictions, the British pressured their government to ban the international slave trade. Parliament passed a law prohibiting the trade in 1807. Over the following decades, Britain successfully pressured Portugal, Spain, France, and Brazil to limit or end their participation in the slave trade. The United Kingdom was able to do this because of its dominance of the seas and its global commercial and political power.

Even imperialism, whose purpose was mainly economic and strategic, needed to be given a humanitarian gloss. Empires claimed to bring the benefits of religion and civilization to the natives. Where the reality diverged too far from the official story, scandals often ensued. Eventually, the imperial powers were forced to publicly rationalize colonization as a temporary expedient, justified only until domestic populations could govern themselves, and no longer. When those populations finally repudiated their imperial masters, imperialism became impossible to sustain as a moral matter.

The nineteenth century also witnessed a series of what we could today call "humanitarian interventions," military actions taken to rescue civilians in foreign countries who were being massacred by their governments or not protected by their governments from atrocities committed by armed groups. Britain, Russia, and France intervened repeatedly in the Balkans to protect Christians from being massacred by mobs or Ottoman troops. These actions often had a strategic role and were rarely perfectly humanitarian—the British were more concerned about Christians being massacred by Ottoman Turks than the other way around, or, for that matter, Christians being massacred by Christians. Nevertheless, actions such as these reflected at least some influence of the humanitarian impulse to help other human beings who were in need regardless of their group membership.

Countries also criticized each other. Western countries criticized Russia for tolerating pogroms that victimized Jews. The persecution of German Jews by the Nazis met with widespread condemnation elsewhere in Europe and North America. After Kristallnacht in 1938, leading figures and media around the world heaped scorn on Germany, accusing the Nazis of "barbarism" and "savagery."

By the eve of World War II, the international moral-legal system had the following characteristics. There was a strong idea, going back to the Peace of Westphalia of 1648, that states were "sovereign," which meant that governments mostly had a free hand to treat their populations however they wanted. This idea had been invoked by governments for centuries, and was based on the hard-won, pragmatic truth that when countries reserve the right to intervene in each other's affairs in order to protect subject populations, warfare is a common outcome. It also played well with the nationalist thinking of the nineteenth century.

But there was also a rough idea that all governments *should* treat their populations humanely, simply by virtue of the fact that their populations consisted of human beings. One could criticize foreign governments for massacring their own citizens, or allowing pogroms, or failing to alleviate famines, or tolerating slavery. In limited cases, especially when the foreign country was weak, or depended on foreign trade, or did not live up to what Europeans regarded as the standard of civilization, a powerful country might use commercial or military force to punish despots and dictators who mistreated their populations. But this was a weak idea, and not embodied in international law as it was then understood.

I.2. THE UNIVERSAL DECLARATION

During World War II, some of the allies, notably the United States and the United Kingdom, justified their war aims in more general terms than self-defense. They sought to repudiate fascism and perhaps any sort of authoritarianism, arguing that governments should be obliged to respect basic civil and political rights and to provide for basic needs. While these general aims received enthusiastic support from political elites in many countries, especially once the war ended, there was, from the start, considerable disagreement about what they would mean in practice. Many allied governments committed atrocities during the war but did not regard themselves (unlike Germany) as having violated international law, and virtually all governments abused citizens in ways that at least echoed Nazi ideas or practices—Jim Crow in the United States, political repression in the colonies of the United Kingdom, and all kinds of repression and misery in the Soviet Union, to name a few.

But these disagreements were swept under the rug at the start, and the United Nations charter provided in a few ambiguous phrases ("reaffirm faith in fundamental human rights" in the Preamble and "assisting in the realization of human rights" in Article 13) that its members would work to advance human rights. A few years later, the General Assembly approved a Universal Declaration of Human Rights. The Universal Declaration provided a long list of rights, most of which are the familiar "negative" or "political" rights that are listed in the U.S. Constitution, or that have been constructed by American courts over the years. The Universal Declaration was not dictated by the United States, however. It reflected the contributions of many different countries, and included rights that were not central to the American national constitutional tradition. Some of those rights were what philosophers call "positive" or "social" rights, including the right

Table 1.1 Selected Provisions of the Universal Declaration of Human Rights

Article	Rights Recognized
Article 3	To life, liberty, and security of person.
Article 5	Not to be subjected to torture or to cruel, inhuman, or degrading treatment or punishment.
Article 10	To a fair and public hearing by an independent and impartial tribunal, in the determination of his rights and obligations and of any criminal charge against him.
Article 17	1. To own property alone as well as in association with others. 2. Not to be arbitrarily deprived of one's property.
Article 18	To freedom of thought, conscience, and religion.
Article 23	1. To work, to free choice of employment, to just and favorable conditions of work, and to protection against unemployment. 2. To equal pay for equal work. 3. To just and favorable remuneration ensuring for himself and his family an existence worthy of human dignity, and supplemented, if necessary, by other means of social protection. 4. To form and to join trade unions for the protection of his interests.
Article 24	To rest and leisure, including reasonable limitation of working hours and periodic holidays with pay.
Article 25	To a standard of living adequate for the health and well-being of himself and of his family, including food, clothing, housing, and medical care and necessary social services, and the right to security in the event of unemployment, sickness, disability, widowhood, old age, or other lack of livelihood in circumstances beyond his control.
Article 27	1. Freely to participate in the cultural life of the community, to enjoy the arts, and to share in scientific advancement and its benefits. 2. To the protection of the moral and material interests resulting from any scientific, literary, or artistic production of which he is the author.

to work, which received a boost from Franklin Roosevelt's "Four Freedoms" speech, but more directly reflected currents in political thought in European and other countries. Table 1.1 lists some of the important rights in the Universal Declaration.

The Universal Declaration was not a treaty in the formal sense: no one at the time believed that it created obligations legally binding on nations. It was not ratified by nations but approved by the General Assembly, and the UN Charter did not give the General Assembly the power to make international law. Moreover, the rights were described in vague, aspirational terms.

This did not auger well for the project of mandating the protection of human rights. Not even the liberal democracies were ready to commit themselves to binding legal obligations. The United States did not commit itself to eliminating Jim Crow, and Great Britain and France did not commit themselves to liberating the subject populations in their colonies. Several authoritarian states—including the Soviet Union, Yugoslavia, Poland, Czechoslovakia, and Saudi Arabia—refused to vote in favor of the Universal Declaration and instead abstained. The words in the Universal Declaration may have been stirring, but no one believed at the time that they portended a major change in the way international relations would be conducted, nor did they capture the imagination of voters, politicians, intellectuals, leaders of political movements, or anyone else who might have exerted political pressure on governments.

1.3. THE COLD WAR ERA

Part of the problem was that a disagreement opened up early on between the United States (as leader of the Western countries) and the Soviet Union (along with its satellites) about the content of human rights. The Americans argued that human rights consisted of political rights—the rights to vote, to speak freely, not to be arbitrarily detained, to practice a religion of one's choice, and the like. These rights were, not coincidentally, the rights in the U.S.

Constitution. The Soviets argued that human rights consisted of social or economic rights—the rights to work, to health care, and to education. Although Stalin's 1936 constitution contained political as well as economic rights, it was plain to everyone by the 1940s that political rights did not exist in the Soviet Union. The Soviets thus argued that human rights consisted of rights associated with work and well-being, and did not include political rights. The Soviets maintained that those rights could be satisfied only by communism; capitalism, they insisted, led to poverty, unemployment, and inequality.

Human rights became yoked to the ideological conflict between the United States and the Soviet Union. And although the language of human rights was used from time to time, everyone understood that the debate was really about the market versus state planning; about democracy versus "dictatorship of the proletariat" or what could most charitably be called rule by a self-perpetuating elite; about God versus atheism. As was so often the case during the Cold War, the conflict was zero-sum. Either you supported political rights (that is, liberal democracy) or you supported economic rights (that is, socialism). The one major human rights treaty the two countries could agree to—the Genocide Convention of 1951, which prohibited countries from engaging in genocides—hardly showed that they shared much common ground. Negotiations to convert the Universal Declaration into a binding treaty were split into two tracks, and it would take another 18 years for the United Nations to adopt a political rights treaty and an economics right treaty, and another decade after that for the treaties to go into force. The result was the International Covenant on Civil and Political Rights (ICCPR) and the International Covenant on Economic, Social, and Cultural Rights (ICESCR), which finally took effect in 1976.

Meanwhile, the United States and the Soviet Union moved toward détente, and in 1975 signed the Helsinki Accords, under which the United States recognized the Soviet Union's control over Eastern Europe, in return for, among other things, Soviet agreement to respect human rights, which led the Soviet Union to ratify the ICCPR in 1976. Dissident groups throughout the Soviet sphere of influence formed Helsinki Watch committees, which reported on human rights violations and pressured Eastern Bloc governments to respect human rights.

In his important book *The Last Utopia*, Samuel Moyn argues that international human rights law did not begin to exercise influence until the mid-1970s, and there is a lot of evidence to support his position if one looks at human rights as a sociological rather than legal phenomenon. Legally, the modern era of human rights began with the Universal Declaration and the recognition that individuals, rather than merely states, possess rights under international law, and thus are entitled to legal protection from abuses by their own governments. Before then, abused populations could appeal to a foreign government for aid, but no one would have said that their appeal was grounded in violations of individual rights.

As Moyn explains, this idea did not become a major force in international relations until the 1970s. It was then that the Helsinki process began; it was a few years later that President Carter announced that human rights would be central to American foreign policy. Congress passed a law in 1977 that conditioned certain types of aid on compliance with human rights norms and required the State Department to issue reports on foreign countries' compliance with those norms. The Helsinki process itself was ambiguous from a human rights perspective, for while the Soviets were forced to agree to respect human rights (mainly at the insistence of the Europeans, not the Americans), it was also widely understood that the West was recognizing Soviet control of Eastern Europe—which meant those countries were condemned to lack democracy and self-determination.

Carter's emphasis on human rights seems to have been a reaction to Vietnam and the gruesome realpolitik of the Nixon/Kissinger era, but Carter himself was unable to maintain a consistent line on human rights. Human-rights violating allies like Iran and Saudi Arabia were just too important for American security, and seen as an important counterweight to Soviet influence, so Carter could not consistently follow through on his rhetoric by threatening to withhold diplomatic support or economic resources from some of the worst violators of human rights.

Still, something changed with Carter. The frequency with which U.S. presidents invoked human rights spiked during the Carter administration, and while subsequent presidents did not emphasize human rights quite as much as Carter did, Carter did effect a lasting change in presidential rhetoric. Carter's five successors—Republicans and Democrats alike—have invoked the term "human rights" far more frequently than any president before Carter. It is not that presidents became more idealistic—Wilson and FDR frequently used idealistic rhetoric. Rather, it is that presidents starting with Carter increasingly began to express their idealistic goals (or to conceal their strategic goals) in the idiom of human rights.

Meanwhile, although Soviet influence was expanding in Africa, Asia, and South America, the ideological basis of Soviet power was beginning to lose its appeal. In the 1970s and 1980s, it became clear that the Soviet system stood not only for political repression (which had been known at least since the 1950s) but also for the failure to deliver economic prosperity. Thus, President Reagan, while not emphasizing human rights as much as President Carter did, nonetheless used them as a cudgel against the Soviets, complaining about their treatment of political dissidents and religious minorities.

The collapse of the Soviet Union was not caused by its human rights violations, or by domestic opposition fueled by those violations. The decline in the price of oil played a much greater role. But with the collapse of the Soviet Union, the major ideological alternative to liberal democracy was gone, and so was the only country that could prevent the United States from imposing its values (for good or ill) on foreign countries.

Three more human rights conventions came into force during this period: the Convention on the Elimination of All Forms of Discrimination Against Women (1979); the Convention Against Torture and Other Cruel, Inhuman or Degrading Treatment or Punishment (1984); and the Convention on the Rights of the Child (1989). With the collapse of communism and the spread of liberal democracy, states joined these and the other human rights treaties in increasing numbers. The most recent treaty is the Convention on the Rights of Persons with Disabilities (2008). Figure 1.1, below, tells the story.

States increasingly appear to regard ratification of the latest human rights treaty—with a few exceptions—as all but compulsory.

It is commonly believed that the West initiated the human rights treaties, and the developing world either followed or resisted. This

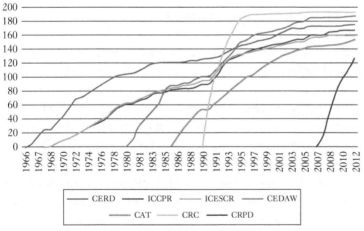

Figure 1.1 Growth of Membership in Seven Major Human Rights Treaties

simplifies a complex story. The general idea of human rights treaties originated in the West, and the rights themselves had been heavily institutionalized in certain Western countries for many years. But many treaties, while heavily influenced by Western norms, were actually initiated by groups in developing countries who hoped to improve rights in those countries and sought outside support. The ICESCR, as we saw, was an effort by the Soviet Union to provide an alternative model to Western-style political rights. But there are other examples as well. The Convention on the Elimination of All Forms of Discrimination Against Women was drafted in response to a UN resolution introduced in 1963 by 22 developing and Eastern European countries. The Convention on the Rights of the Child was initially proposed by Poland and other Soviet bloc countries. And while the Convention on the Rights of Persons with Disabilities can be traced back to a proposal made by Sweden and Italy in 1987, Mexico, Jordan, South Africa, and many other developing countries played a prominent role in its negotiation—while the major Western countries had to be dragged along.

1.4. THE MODERN ERA

By the 1990s, it was possible to argue that there really was an international human rights "regime," in the sense that there was something like a consensus among nations that all countries must respect human rights, despite considerable disagreement as to what this meant. Not all countries had ratified all the treaties; but most countries had ratified most of the treaties. (Today, each of the six major human rights treaties has been ratified by more than 150 countries, and some treaties—including the ICCPR and the Rights of the Child Convention—have been ratified by nearly all countries.) Nor was there agreement about all the rights and what they meant, but most countries seemed to agree about many of the rights.

Some legal theorists began talking about a global constitution or international bill of rights—higher law that superseded domestic law and other forms of international law, and that states could not withdraw from. Others argued that human rights had entered customary international law, a body of law that was thought to bind states even though it was not embodied in treaties, because states gave their implicit (or explicit) consent to particular norms. On this view, norms in treaties reflected customary international law and hence bound even states that had not ratified those treaties.

However, this view emerged at the same time that events made a mockery of it. One was the horrifying genocide in Rwanda, where in a matter of months in 1994, members of the Hutu majority slaughtered more than 800,000 members of the Tutsi minority along with their Hutu supporters. Other countries stood by when they could have intervened and stopped it. The other event was the civil war in Yugoslavia, which featured significant civilian massacres as well as other atrocities. The civil war was not worse than other civil wars that had taken place in Asia, Latin America, and Africa during the Cold War and after, but it struck a nerve because it took place in Europe. Foreign countries did intervene, albeit slowly.

Human rights supporters could take comfort in the fact that, while the United Nations responded slowly, it set up international tribunals to try the worst perpetrators of atrocities in Rwanda and the former Yugoslavia. These criminal trials revived the idea, which had been defunct since the Nuremberg and Tokyo trials after World War II, that individuals could commit international crimes by engaging in human rights violations that exceeded an ambiguous threshold of atrocity. The tribunals were not entirely successful. They were enormously expensive, and resources were only enough to try a small handful of the perpetrators. Some of the doctrines that they developed to facilitate conviction were criticized for relying on guilt by association, and all factions believed that the tribunals were biased against them. A new controversy has recently erupted over whether the Yugoslavia tribunal is cutting back on criminal liability.

Unhappiness with the tribunals led to the establishment of the International Criminal Court in 1998, which gained general jurisdiction over all international crimes committed in a member country or by a national of a member country. But the ICC has experienced significant growing pains since it began operations in 2002. It has tried very few people, and it has taken jurisdiction only over African countries, which has led to accusations of bias even though several of those countries sought ICC intervention.

More to the point, human rights law never became a consistent factor in U.S. foreign policy. The United States continued to tolerate human rights violations by important allies. No president after Carter made human rights as central to his foreign policy rhetoric as Carter did. Still, the 1990s were the high-water mark for human rights. With the collapse of the Soviet Union, economic and social rights lost their stigmatizing association with communism and entered the constitutional law of many Western countries, with the result that all major issues of public policy were increasingly seen as shaped by human rights. Human rights played an increasingly important role in the European Union, although the focus there was always on internal consolidation. Members of the European Union respected human rights as a matter of domestic constitutional law, but they also recognized an increasing role for human rights in European law, and insisted that countries that sought to join the EU in order to obtain the economic benefits of being part of the union be required to respect human rights as well. At the same time, the EU has never put significant resources into advancing human rights outside of Europe. The activity of NGOs devoted to advancing human rights as they defined them also increased during this period. And many countries that emerged from under the Soviet yoke adopted

Western constitutional systems—even Russia itself made halting movements in that direction.

Then came September 11, 2001. America's recourse to torture was a significant challenge to the human rights regime. Human rights advocates tried to attribute it to a wayward Republican administration, but the fact is that many Americans supported the use of torture. Most polls of Americans between 2001 and 2009 found that a substantial portion of the population (between 15 percent and 54 percent) was in favor of torture. Governments of other countries, including traditional liberal countries like those of Western Europe, were complicit in U.S. torture. In February of 2013, the Open Society Justice Initiative released a report accusing 54 countries, including major European countries like Germany and the United Kingdom, of participating in the torture and abuse of detainees in the U.S. extraordinary rendition program. The detention center at Guantanamo Bay also posed a challenge to the spirit of the human rights treaties, although indefinite detentions and military tribunals pose a closer legal question than torture does. As long as the conflict with Al Qaeda could be classified as a "war" (a controversial but not clearly wrong view), then those institutions could be justified under the laws of war. Torture, however, could not be justified under the laws of war or human rights law.

What was striking and awkward for human rights supporters is that the United States was a traditional leader in human rights, and one of only a few countries that has used its power and resources to advance human rights in other nations. Moreover, the prohibition on torture is at the core of the human rights regime; if that right is less than absolute, then surely the other rights are as well. Many commentators, foreign governments, and NGOs criticized the United States for engaging in torture, and the U.S. government eventually backed down. It remains unclear, however, why it backed down, and whether or not it was influenced by this criticism.

Moreover, many countries remain hostile to human rights. Foremost among them is China, the most dynamic country in the world, which is on the cusp of superpower status. China has worked quietly but assiduously behind the scenes to weaken international human rights institutions and, more noisily, to reject international criticism of the political repression of its citizens. It has offered diplomatic and economic support to human-rights violators like Sudan, which Western countries have tried to isolate. Along with Russia, it has used its veto in the Security Council to limit Western efforts to advance human rights through economic pressure and military intervention. And it has joined with numerous other countries hostile to human rights—major emerging powers like Vietnam, and Islamic countries that fear Western secularization—to deny many of the core values that human rights are supposed to protect.

This raises the question of how much human rights *law* has actually influenced the behavior of countries. In one view, the answer is quite a bit. As I have described, most countries have ratified the majority of the most important human rights treaties. Today, when governments criticize each other, they frequently invoke the language of human rights. NGOs that advocate human rights have proliferated; Amnesty International and Human Rights Watch are just the most prominent of hundreds of organizations. The media discuss their reports. Numerous UN organizations monitor human rights, and there are regional courts that enforce human rights law, most notably the European Court of Human Rights. Law schools teach human rights law. There is even private litigation in America based on international human rights violations. None of this was true 50 years ago.

And yet there is a nagging question as to whether all of this activity has actually improved people's lives. It turns out that this question is hard to answer. In a very rough sense, the world is a freer place than it was 50 years ago, but is it freer because of the human rights treaties or because of other events—such as economic growth or the collapse of communism? In Chapter 4, I will discuss the evidence that human rights treaties have improved respect for human rights in detail, but the bottom line for present purposes is that if they have, the effect has been small; plus, as I will explain, it is hard to rule out offsetting factors that have negated any existing positive effects.

CHAPTER TWO

The Law and Institutions of Human Rights

2.1. THE PROLIFERATION OF TREATIES

Many treaties touch on human rights in various ways, but nine treaties are generally regarded as "core" human rights treaties. They are listed below in Table 2.1, along with the year in which they went into force, and the number of states that have ratified them as of January 2013.

All of these treaties have certain common features. They commit states to respect an assortment of human rights and generally require states to incorporate these rights into domestic law. They set up committees that monitor compliance but lack authority to order states to comply. Some of the treaties are accompanied by optional protocols, which create additional rights or obligations (the Second Optional Protocol of the ICCPR bans the death penalty) or additional institutional machinery for ensuring compliance (the First Optional Protocol of the ICCPR provides individuals a means for filing complaints against their governments).

Table 2.1 Core Human Rights Treaties

Treaty	Adoption by General Assembly	Entry into force	Number of ratifying states as of Jan., 2013
International Convention on the Elimination of All Forms of Racial Discrimination (ICERD)	1965	1969	176
International Covenant on Civil and Political Rights (ICCPR)	1966	1976	167
International Covenant on Economic, Social and Cultural Rights (ICESCR)	1966	1976	160
Convention on the Elimination of All Forms of Discrimination Against Women (ICEDAW)	1979	1981	187
Convention Against Torture and Other Cruel, Inhuman or Degrading Treatment or Punishment (CAT)	1984	1987	153
Convention on the Rights of the Child (CRC)	1989	1990	193
International Convention on the Protection of the Rights of All Migrant Workers and Members of Their Families (ICRMW)	1990	2003	46
International Convention for the Protection of All Persons from Enforced Disappearance (ICPPED)	2006	2010	39
Convention on the Rights of Persons with Disabilities (CRPD)	2006	2008	132

The substantive provisions of the treaties can be gleaned from their titles. The ICCPR recognizes a large number of political and civil rights, similar to those that appear in the U.S. Bill of Rights and that have long been recognized in liberal democracies. These rights include the right to free speech, to the free exercise of religion, to join associations, to be tried by an independent judge, not to be arbitrarily detained, not to be searched without cause, and so on. However, in a major respect the ICCPR, as interpreted by many countries, goes beyond U.S. constitutional law, requiring the government to take affirmative steps to stop human rights violations by private persons. For example, Article 6, which provides that "Every human being has the inherent right to life," has been interpreted to impose a positive duty on governments to protect people's lives by regulating industrial workplaces and by supplying police protection from crime.

The ICESCR contains a small number of mainly economic rights, including the right to work, the right to be paid a fair wage, the right to vacations, the right to education, the right to health care, and the right to welfare or old-age pensions. CEDAW prohibits sex discrimination, providing, for example, that women have the same access to the franchise, education, work, and health care as men do. CAT bans torture, both as a means for extracting information and for punishing people, and includes provisions banning cruel and inhuman punishments that fall short of torture. CRC requires states to act in the best interest of children, not to separate them from their families except in narrow circumstances, not to permit them to be abused or neglected, to ensure that they can express themselves freely and exercise their freely chosen religion, and so on. ICRMW extends the ICCPR rights to migrant workers to the extent consistent with their status as non-citizens. ICPPED focuses on the specific problem of governments that make their opponents "disappear," that is, that detain or kill them without giving public notice. The Convention bans this practice and requires states to implement laws to ensure that governments do not backslide. CRPD prohibits discrimination against persons with disabilities and requires states to ensure that employers and others accommodate their disabilities. A list of the treaties can be found in Table 2.1.

The overall human rights legal regime may seem like a mess, but a simple pattern emerges. Human rights include the basic classical liberal ("negative") rights of political participation and personal security against arbitrary government action, plus so-called positive rights to security, education, medical care, work, and so forth, which are today associated with social democracy in Europe. The various non-discrimination treaties provide that states must extend these rights to women, children, refugees, and disabled people, and may also be required to make further accommodations to the special circumstances of these people where appropriate.

This picture should be familiar. The United States, the European countries, Australia, Canada—all the major developed countries—have long recognized such rights for their citizens. That is not to say that all of them recognize these rights as constitutional rights, but in all these countries a significant portion of public policy is devoted to ensuring that these rights are respected. Even in the United States, which is often considered a laggard among the developed nations, and where the language of positive rights is politically controversial, all children are entitled to public schooling, nearly everyone has access to health care, and the government tries to keep the unemployment rate as low as possible. Indeed, U.S. state constitutions contain numerous positive rights; the emphasis on political rights in the national constitution makes the U.S. constitutional tradition seem more libertarian than it really is.

So, in one sense, the human rights treaties do not require the developed countries to do anything different from what they have done in the past. To be sure, the treaties prohibit these countries from repudiating these rights—and that is what got the United States into trouble when it started torturing Al Qaeda detainees after 9/11. Moreover, the treaties are written in general terms, and it is possible to interpret them broadly enough so as to create new rights that countries had not previously recognized. For example, if international institutions and most countries come to believe that the prohibition on torture and cruel and inhuman punishment also encompasses the death penalty because the death penalty is cruel and akin to torture, then the Torture Convention might require countries to abandon the death penalty—at least in theory. As we will see below, however, there is no clear institutional mechanism for generating such new interpretations.

By contrast, the human rights treaties impose significant burdens on authoritarian states, as well as poor and developing states, which as a practical matter, whatever the intentions of government officials, are not wealthy enough or well organized enough to comply with the treaty obligations. Nearly all countries have ratified the ICCPR, yet Freedom House classifies 47 states as "not free," which implies that they violate ICCPR rights to freedom of expression, participation in government, and protection from arbitrary detention. Why did authoritarian countries ratify the ICCPR, and why hasn't the ICCPR forced them to become democracies? This is a question that we will return to later in this book.

The broad outlines of the human rights treaties should now be clear. Let us now narrow the focus and fill in some details. From Article 19 of the ICCPR:

2. Everyone shall have the right to freedom of expression; this right shall include freedom to seek, receive and impart information and ideas of all kinds, regardless of frontiers, either orally, in writing or in print, in the form of art, or through any other media of his choice.
3. The exercise of the rights provided for in paragraph 2 of this article carries with it special duties and responsibilities. It may therefore be subject to certain restrictions, but these shall only be such as are provided by law and are necessary:

(a) For respect of the rights or reputations of others;

(b) For the protection of national security or of public order (ordre public), or of public health or morals.

Anyone familiar with the jurisprudence that has grown up around the First Amendment of the U.S. Constitution knows that phrases like these are not self-defining. Even though the U.S. Constitution lacks a qualifying clause like section (3), the courts have read countless limitations into the right to freedom of expression, so that restrictions can be put on fraudulent, misleading, commercial, defamatory, obscene, and dangerous speech. The explicit recognition in the ICCPR that speech can be limited for the protection of national security, public order, and public morals could lead to restrictions on speech that is protected in the United States, including criticism of the government, criticism of religious norms and other dominant social norms, and criticism of public officials. In short, the ICCPR right to freedom of expression is too vague to rule out significant constraints on expression, including many that would be clearly objectionable from a U.S. (or even broadly Western) perspective.

To take another example, consider the ICESCR's provisions on the right to work:

Article 6

1. The States Parties to the present Covenant recognize the right to work, which includes the right of everyone to the opportunity to gain his living by work which he freely chooses or accepts, and will take appropriate steps to safeguard this right.

2. The steps to be taken by a State Party to the present Covenant to achieve the full realization of this right shall include technical and vocational guidance and training programmes, policies and techniques to achieve steady economic, social and cultural

development and full and productive employment under conditions safeguarding fundamental political and economic freedoms to the individual.

Article 7

The States Parties to the present Covenant recognize the right of everyone to the enjoyment of just and favourable conditions of work which ensure, in particular:

(a) Remuneration which provides all workers, as a minimum, with:
    (i) Fair wages and equal remuneration for work of equal value without distinction of any kind, in particular women being guaranteed conditions of work not inferior to those enjoyed by men, with equal pay for equal work;
    (ii) A decent living for themselves and their families in accordance with the provisions of the present Covenant;
(b) Safe and healthy working conditions;
(c) Equal opportunity for everyone to be promoted in his employment to an appropriate higher level, subject to no considerations other than those of seniority and competence;
(d) Rest, leisure and reasonable limitation of working hours and periodic holidays with pay, as well as remuneration for public holidays.

These articles raise numerous interpretive difficulties (what are "fair" wages, what is a "decent" living, what is a "reasonable" limitation of working hours?), but the most serious problem is that they treat work as something that the state can dole out. In fact, ensuring full employment is one of the greatest challenges of macroeconomic policy, and requires extremely difficult tradeoffs. Many countries have been willing to tolerate high unemployment rates because they appear to be an unavoidable consequence of social welfare programs, which discourage people from seeking employment (and which appear to be required by Articles 9 and 11). Governments can trade off short-term and long-term goals—for example, by lowering interest rates, a government can ensure a high level of employment today, but it then takes the risk that inflation in the future will cause economic disruptions that reduce employment. It is difficult to imagine how one would ascertain whether a government has satisfied or failed to satisfy the right to work.

In recent years, unemployment in many European countries has been extremely high. The unemployment rate in Spain in 2012, for example, was over 25 percent. Most economists attribute these high unemployment rates to rigid labor markets. Laws make it difficult for employers to fire workers, so employers are afraid to hire them in the first place. Thus, did Spain violate the right to work in the ICESCR by failing to liberalize its labor markets? Or could Spain justly argue that labor market regulations served other legitimate values? Again, it is hard to imagine how one could answer these questions, at least without drawing on general public policy views and moral and political commitments that are not set out in the ICESCR.

For developing countries, these problems are even more acute. A government of a poor country may want to provide medical care to its population but lack the resources to do so. The ICESCR's drafters recognized this problem. Article 2 provides that "Each State Party to the present Covenant undertakes to take steps, individually and through international assistance and co-operation, especially economic and technical, to the maximum of its available resources, with a view to achieving progressively the full realization of the rights recognized in the present Covenant by all appropriate means." Thus, poor countries may disregard economic rights as long as they can claim that they hope to satisfy them in the future. Article 4, which applies to all countries rather than just developing countries, provides that the rights in the ICESCR may be limited for "the purpose of promoting the general welfare." Even wealthy countries can thus argue that their failure to satisfy economic rights may be justified by other concerns, as in the case of Spain. But then what is left of the rights themselves?

Consider a few clauses from the Convention on the Rights of the Child. Article 11(1) provides that "States Parties shall take measures to combat the illicit transfer and non-return of children abroad." But it does not identify those measures, and so it would be difficult to accuse a state of violating this provision unless it did literally nothing. Article 12(1) provides "States Parties shall assure to the child who is capable of forming his or her own views the right to express those views freely in all matters affecting the child, the views of the child being given due weight in accordance with the age and maturity of the child." Here, again, the Convention is vague on crucial matters, such as the relationship between the age or maturity of the child and what the child is allowed to say. A similar point can be made about Article 19(1): "States Parties shall take all appropriate legislative, administrative, social and educational measures to protect the child from all forms of physical or mental violence, injury or abuse, neglect or negligent treatment, maltreatment or exploitation, including sexual abuse, while in the care of parent(s), legal guardian(s) or any other person who has the care of the child." Which measures are "appropriate"? What is "neglect"? Such vagueness pervades the Convention.

To add to the complexity, countries that enter into these treaties frequently include reservations, understandings, and declarations—collectively known as RUDs—which limit or modify their treaty obligations. Some reservations specifically negate a treaty obligation as it applies to the reserving state. Article 37(c) of the Convention on the Rights of the Child and Article 10(2) of the ICCPR require states to segregate juvenile and adult prisoners; many countries, including Switzerland, the Netherlands, Australia, the United Kingdom, and the United States, declared that they will not comply with this provision when it is not feasible to do so. An Islamic country, such as Afghanistan, Iran, Egypt, or Saudi Arabia, might state that it interprets articles of the CRC and ICEDAW so that they are consistent with Islamic law; European countries may say that they will interpret the treaty so that it is consistent with the European Convention on Human Rights, as Austria and Belgium did in agreeing to the CRC; the United States will say that the treaty must be consistent with the U.S. Constitution. Many countries say that the treaty, or particular articles, will be interpreted consistently with their laws. The Republic of Korea, for instance, declared that Article 22 of the ICCPR, which protects the right of freedom of association, "shall be so applied as to be in conformity with the provisions of the local laws including the Constitution of the Republic of Korea."

Perhaps surprisingly, RUDs are more frequently issued by democracies than by non-democracies. One might think that non-democracies would issue RUDs so that they would limit their risk of being found in violation of a treaty. But democracies take their legal obligations more seriously than non-democracies do, and they issue RUDs to ensure that they do not take on obligations that they cannot comply with. By contrast, non-democracies are more apt to treat human rights treaties as propaganda; issuing RUDs that hollow out the core of their treaty obligations would defeat the purpose of assuring the world that they respect human rights.

Another complication is that some human rights exist outside any formal treaty. Most famously, the "right to development" was advanced by developing countries including China and endorsed by the General Assembly. The right to development is the right to economic growth, seen to be necessary for people living in poor countries. Human rights campaigners worry that states will invoke the right to development to rationalize violations of political freedoms. Indeed, China argues that the right to development—the right of people to eventually be free from poverty—justifies restrictions on political freedoms. China purports to balance personal and political freedoms against poverty reduction; the right to development allows it to do so without departing from the idiom of human rights.

In a similar vein, recent years have also seen the emergence of a "right to security." A 2005 UN document defines the right to security as "the right of people to live in freedom and dignity, free from poverty and despair," a right that includes for all people "freedom from fear and freedom from want, with an equal opportunity to enjoy all their rights and fully develop their human potential." One scholar, after surveying global discussions of this right, observes:

> [T]he right to security can protect dignity, equality, liberty, physical and psychological autonomy, freedom from fear and freedom from want. The range of goods and interests this right promises to protect is extensive, and we are left with the sneaking suspicion that the right to security can be deployed to protect most things that we want in life.[1]

The same scholar worries that the right to security will devour human rights protections by enabling states to justify restrictions on personal freedom. Indeed, governments have cited the right to security in just this way, invoking their duty to protect people's right to be free of crime, terrorism, and military attack, in order to justify restrictions on civil liberties. Just as with the right to development, states justify what they regard as reasonable balancing among security and liberty interests without departing from the idiom of human rights.

2.2. THE UN COMMITTEES, COUNCIL, AND HIGH
COMMISSION

Ambiguities in the human rights treaties need not be alarming. The domestic law of all countries overflows with ambiguities. Legal institutions, including courts and regulatory agencies, play a crucial role in filling gaps in the law. Depending on the legal tradition or the institution, those agents may see their role as gleaning the intention of the lawmakers or as drawing on policy considerations or moral norms, or a combination. Thus, ambiguous provisions are given specificity over time, and people can predict how agents will interpret them based on the agents' past decisions, so provisions that start off as ambiguous can nonetheless provide the type of guidance that is crucial for the rule of law.

The U.S. Constitution contains numerous vague provisions. The First Amendment provides that "Congress shall make no law...abridging the freedom of speech, or of the press; or the right of the people peaceably to assemble, and to petition the Government for a redress of grievances." Over the years, courts and other institutions have glossed the text beyond recognition—so that it does not block laws against defamation, incitement to violence, fraud, obscenity, and the disclosure of national security secrets. Nor does it block "reasonable" regulations that ensure that protest marches are not excessively disruptive. It has also been expanded so that it applies to the executive branch, state governments, and other entities aside from Congress. Many of these interpretations were initially controversial, and some still are, but they have all been accepted because of a strong norm that interpretations by the Supreme Court bind the national and state governments.

The originators of the human rights treaties recognized this role for legal institutions, and sought to build them. But they ran into resistance from states, for while states were willing to enter into human rights treaties, they have been much more reluctant about submitting to the jurisdiction of courts or other legal bodies. The resulting international legal institutions are thus considerably weaker than domestic legal institutions. I will provide a quick survey of these international institutions and then comment on this state of affairs.

There are three types of international institutions devoted to human rights issues. First, each of the major human rights treaties comes with its own "committee," which is given the responsibility for ensuring that states comply with the treaty. Thus, there is a Human Rights Committee associated with the ICCPR; a Committee on Economic, Social, and Cultural Rights associated with the ICESCR; a Committee on the Elimination of Racial Discrimination associated with the CERD; a Committee on the Rights of the Child associated with the treaty of that name; and so on. Second, a UN Council on Human Rights (the successor of the UN Commission on Human Rights) has authority to monitor compliance with all the human rights treaties. Third, the United Nations also has an Office of the High Commissioner for Human Rights, whose occupant has vaguely defined responsibilities relating to human rights but seems to be understood as an official spokesperson for UN policy toward human rights.

Human Rights Committees. There are 10 human rights committees, each associated with one of nine human rights treaties (and one associated with an optional protocol of one of the treaties). Each committee has 10 to 25 members, who are nationals of states that belong to the treaties and are elected by secret ballot. The major responsibilities of the committees are to provide guidance to countries and interpretations of the treaties and to review periodic reports submitted by the parties to the treaties.

The committees have dutifully issued recommendations over the years; their reports now number in the dozens. The committees urge states to collect and report data, to apply treaty norms to new developments, or just to comply with treaty norms. They sometimes criticize reservations. The CCPR committee has encouraged states not to derogate from the ICCPR; argued that the "right to life" obligates states to reduce infant mortality and increase life expectancy; claimed that solitary confinement can be torture; attempted to limit pretrial detention; and called for states to eliminate nuclear weapons.

The committees also review the periodic reports issued by nations, and can use these reviews as an opportunity to advance interpretations of the treaties. In its report, a nation explains how it implements the treaty. The committee then makes observations on the report, sometimes on the basis of independently collected information. Seven of the committees were given the authority to receive petitions from individuals who believe that their human rights have been violated if the relevant nation has ratified the relevant protocol. Committees do not adjudicate these petitions, but may invite nations to respond to the complaints, and attempt to mediate a resolution. Six of the committees were given the authority to initiate country inquiries, where particular countries are singled out for investigation because of evidence of systematic violations. Again, the committees do not act as judges or enforcement authorities, but can initiate a dialogue with the country, albeit only if the country cooperates.

The committees are weak, and their reports overflow with sensible bromides that everyone can agree with but are unlikely to lead to specific action. The committees often identify general social problems and throw off vague suggestions as to how they could be addressed. Here are some quotations from a collection of committee reports on Finland. "Continue strengthening legal and institutional mechanisms aimed at combating discrimination." "Increase efforts to implement effectively current policies aimed at combating violence." "Ensure that adequate resources are afforded to public health services." "Examine extent to which human rights education is available in schools." "Continue the efforts to monitor all tendencies which may give rise to racist and xenophobic behavior." The Finns are surely already aware of these problems and will have no doubt taken steps to address them consistent with limited resources and other priorities.

The committee system is not taken seriously by the nations. As of 2011, only 16 percent of countries had provided their periodic reports on time. Twenty percent have never submitted a report under the ICESCR, Convention Against Torture, and ICCPR. There are major backlogs. Part of the problem may be the sheer number of committees and their overlapping jurisdictions. In addition, the committees have vast jurisdiction over most of the world while possessing few resources, which of course limits their effectiveness. They can accomplish little without the cooperation of the nations that they investigate, which further limits their ability to do good.

As noted, seven of the committees can hear petitions from individuals or groups who claim that a government has violated a provision of the treaty that the committee administers. The committees obtain jurisdiction over a country only if that country ratifies a separate optional protocol, which countries have done in large numbers. Yet the committees do not have the power to issue sanctions or remedies, or even to issue official legally binding judgments; typically, they try to enter into a "dialogue" with the offending country. What this means in practice is that victims of human rights abuses and their advocates do not see much point in using the committee system. The Human Rights Committee—the committee associated with the ICCPR—has received 1,677 petitions since 1976, or about 45 per year. The Committee found violations in 809 cases and received a "satisfactory response" from the country in only 67 of them. The Committee Against Torture—the committee associated with the Convention Against Torture—has heard only 284 petitions since 1990, or only about 12 per year. The Committee found violations in 76 cases, and received a "satisfactory response" from the country in 37 of them. Only 26 cases have been brought to the CEDAW committee since 2004. The committee found violations in 13 cases, received a "satisfactory response" in 4, and is engaged in dialogue in the others. Only 50 cases have been brought to the CERD committee since 1988. The committee found violations in 14 cases, and received a satisfactory response in 4. The lack of a "satisfactory response" does not literally mean noncompliance, as often a "dialogue" is taking place. Still, it seems impossible that the infinitesimal prospect of being brought before one of these committees by a victim of human rights violations could affect government policy or the behavior of government officials.

The problems with the committee system are well known. In 2012 the UN High Commissioner on Human Rights issued a report on the Human Rights Committee—possibly the best and most respected of the 10 committees—that pointed out its many deficiencies and concluded that, as a result of a "long history of benign neglect," the Committee is "on the verge of drowning in its growing workload."[2] But as Yuval Shany points out, the report's proposals for streamlining and other efficiency—promoting measures ignore the "'elephant in the room'—namely, what appears to be a conscious decision by a significant number of state-parties to maintain the treaty bodies under permanent conditions of under-effectiveness."[3] He continues: "The unhappy situation of the UN treaty bodies may thus be explained in large part by a tension between a superficial commitment by many state-parties to the goal of human rights promotion and a *realpolitik* aversion to actual treaty implementation."[4]

The UN Council on Human Rights. The UN Council on Human Rights, like the committees, has the power to monitor compliance with human rights treaties. But, unlike the committees, its remit is general, not tied to any specific treaty. It can provide an overall evaluation of a country's respect for human rights. In addition, the

Council is a higher profile body. Its members are governments (acting through delegates) rather than experts, and its deliberations and resolutions are more likely to find their way into news reports than those of the committees.

The Council was originally called the UN Commission on Human Rights. The Commission's first major act was to draft the Universal Declaration of Human Rights. But it was less successful at monitoring countries or developing the law. Like other UN institutions, it did little during the Cold War. And by the 2000s, it was beset by criticisms from all sides.

Critics made several objections. First, many of the members of the Commission were the worst human rights violators, including Libya, Saudi Arabia, and Sudan. Second, and as a result, the Commission did not criticize the worst human rights violators, and indeed hardly any at all. The human rights violators formed alliances with each other, and with other countries that cared more about diplomatic or strategic cooperation than about human rights, and used these coalitions to shield themselves from criticism. Third, where the Commission was able to criticize, it directed its criticism mostly at Israel. And while Israel may have deserved criticism, it did not deserve to be picked on to the exclusion of North Korea, Sudan, and Myanmar. Fourth, Islamic countries repeatedly put on the agenda the theory of "defamation of religion"—that criticisms of religion, such as the cartoons depicting Muhammad, violated the human rights of religious believers. The West firmly rejected this view, but found itself outvoted time and again.

This doesn't mean that the Commission acted in an entirely arbitrary way, or was completely beholden to the most powerful countries or the best-organized coalition. It did provide a forum for criticizing repressive countries. An adverse resolution from the Commission could reduce a country's chance of receiving multilateral aid. But there is no evidence it changed any target country's behavior.

In 2006 the United Nations abolished the Commission and replaced it with the UN Human Rights Council—in other words, it reorganized the Commission and gave it a new name. It tried to limit membership to countries that respected human rights, and introduced some other reforms, including a process for suspending members who commit human rights violations. But the Council has turned out to be not much different from the Commission. Human rights abusers continue to populate its membership, albeit in lower numbers than before. It has widened its scope of criticism, but still focuses on Israel and ignores many countries with worse human rights records.

According to Freedom House's 2009–2010 report card, "The Council did not issue a resolution on Iran, despite evidence of massive human rights violations in that country throughout the year, and no resolutions were passed to address ongoing systematic abuses in countries such as Belarus, China, Cuba, Libya, Saudi Arabia, Sudan, and Syria."[5] In addition, and probably most troublesome, the procedures for monitoring seem designed to avoid embarrassing the countries. The Universal Periodic Review Procedure ensures that all countries are subject to monitoring—so the worst violators are not singled out. And it allows countries to register their objections about the conduct of the country under review, which they do in diplomacy-speak. The report does not provide a consensus view on the country's human rights record, and so lacks political salience. In the words of Freedom House, "States such as Iran that are not interested in reform undermine the process by presenting preposterously positive reports about their records and lining up friendly countries to testify on their behalf."[6]

If you read the Universal Periodic Review reports, it is possible to feel a sense of progress. South Africa agreed in 2008 to improve access to HIV/AIDS treatment and to prohibit corporal punishment in schools, and by 2012 it had done so. In response to recommendations in the 2008 report, Indonesia passed laws protecting freedom of expression and prohibiting racial and ethnic discrimination, and improved human rights training for police forces. But these improvements were mostly on paper; there is some dispute over the magnitude of the changes, and not much evidence. Moreover, given that these states agreed to these recommendations, it is likely that they were already on the domestic political agenda, and there is little reason to believe that the Universal Periodic Review made much of a difference. Finally, the states failed to make progress on a huge range of issues—from torture to human trafficking.

One of the most highly regarded programs of the Council is the system of "special procedures," which refers to the practice of giving mandates to individual experts or small committees of experts from outside the UN system, who are asked to investigate human rights problems in particular countries or address certain issues or themes that transcend specific countries. The expert or committee finds facts and writes reports, which are then submitted to the Council or the General Assembly and communicated to relevant countries. In recent years, the Council has authorized country reports on Sudan, Iran, Côte d'Ivoire, Syria, Belarus, Eritrea, Mali, and the Central African Republic, and thematic reports on issues including slavery, water sanitation, cultural rights, discrimination against women, transnational corporations, the environment, and the human rights of elderly persons. Some of these reports received public attention and led to further diplomatic developments, but it is unknown whether concrete progress in human rights resulted.

The evidence on the first few years of its performance indicates that the Council has continued the legacy of the Commission. Governments that abuse human rights covet seats on the Council, so that they can use their votes to deflect attention from their own abuses or sell them in return for financial or diplomatic assistance, which they use to shore up their position at home.

The Office of the United Nations High Commissioner for Human Rights. The OHCHR was created in 1993, motivated by the worry that the numerous human rights bodies lacked coordination and needed leadership. But the OHCHR does not have any legal authority; it is a political office charged with a mandate to improve human rights everywhere. The office sends out representatives to various hot spots where systematic human rights violations are occurring, and tries to mediate among conflicting parties and provide help to victims. The OHCHR also serves as the secretariat for the Human Rights Council and assists it in its various functions; provides administrative support to the human rights committees; gives countries advice regarding human rights standards; pressures other UN agencies to advance human rights; and serves as a roving human rights advocate and educator. Little has been written about the OHCHR and its role in enforcing human rights law.

It is possible that some of these bodies have done some good by embarrassing countries that have violated human rights, but the important point for present purposes is that they do not fill the role, akin to that of a domestic court, of giving content or specificity to the vague human rights norms. The bodies either fail to advance interpretations of the law, or they advance interpretations that countries do not accept. Because they lack any legal authority, they are in no position to claim that their interpretations must prevail, and they cannot compel countries to adopt them or obey them. Why don't countries give them more power? We will see, when we turn to the European Court of Human Rights, that a powerful human rights body exists. But the experience of that Court will also help explain why countries refuse to create a similar body at the international level.

2.3. THE EUROPEAN COURT AND OTHER REGIONAL BODIES

Three major regional human rights courts exist—in Latin America, in Africa, and in Europe. Of these, the European Court of Human Rights is by far the most prominent, and so I will focus on it. The Court enforces the European Convention for the Protection of Human Rights and Fundamental Freedoms, which went into force in 1953. The European Convention incorporates many of the human rights that are detailed in the international human rights treaties that I have discussed. Today, 47 states belong to the Convention, including Russia, Ukraine, and Turkey. The Convention, as amended by various protocols, permits individuals to bring claims directly against the governments of the member states. If the Court rules in favor of a complainant, it can order the government to pay damages, but it cannot strike down the offending law. Another body known as the Committee of Ministers monitors compliance, and puts pressure on states that fail to bring their laws into conformity with the Court's interpretation of the Convention.

The salient fact about the Court is that it comprises 47 judges—one from each member state of the Council of Europe—and has jurisdiction over 800 million people. It does not hear appeals from lower courts; there are no lower courts. Tens of thousands of new cases are brought every year, and the backlog was more than 113,000 cases in 2012. Because the Court cannot strike down domestic laws, each decision has limited effect—bringing a remedy to a single person or possibly group—although states are under pressure to change laws that the Court has deemed in violation of the Convention.

The first thing that must be understood, then, is that the Court lacks the resources to provide justice for more than a tiny fraction of the millions of people under its jurisdiction. This might not be a problem if the Court ruled over only liberal democracies like Germany and Denmark, but it also rules over Russia, Turkey, and Ukraine. In recent years, it has dealt with between 40,000 and 90,000 applications per year, declaring most of them inadmissible. It rendered judgments in fewer than 3,000 cases per year and issued monetary awards in about 500 to 700 cases per year. The monetary awards are miniscule, with most of them under 10,000 euros, even for very serious abuses; one was 50,000 euros (for a detainee who was tortured and sodomized with a truncheon); and one was 378,000 euros (for a person who was infected by HIV at birth as a result of government misbehavior, and then denied health care provided by law). Thus, even the worst human rights abusing countries know that they will never pay in aggregate more than a few million euros per year under the ECHR system, the tiniest of pinpricks to their national budgets, thanks to the ECHR's limited capacity and the tradition of small awards.

Generally speaking, countries—particularly liberal democracies—comply with the Court's judgments, although often grudgingly and narrowly. But some recent empirical studies have cast doubts on the Court's overall effectiveness. One found that only 58 percent of judgments between 1960 and 2005 were resolved or closed by November 2009; another found a 48-percent compliance rate.[7] Many of the countries under the Court's jurisdiction—including Azerbaijan, Russia, Ukraine, Armenia, Turkey, Albania, and Georgia—are not models of human rights. All of these countries were classified as "not free" or "partly free" by Freedom House in 2012. Russia, in particular, has been an embarrassment for the ECHR. In 1991, after the collapse of the Soviet Union, Russia received Freedom House rankings of 3 for political rights and 3 for civil liberties—earning the label "partly free." (The scale ranges from 1 (best) to 7 (worst).) Its rankings had worsened, to 4 and 4, by the time it ratified the European Convention on Human Rights in 1998.[8] Since then, Russia's rankings have further worsened to 6 for political rights and 5 for civil liberties. Freedom House now declares Russia "not free." By contrast, most of the other members of the ECHR have maintained scores in the 1 to 2 range during this entire period.

The causes of Russia's return to authoritarianism are many. The chaotic transition in the 1990s brought widespread economic distress, cultural malaise, and the loss of foreign influence and prestige. Vladimir Putin, who came to power in 2000, promised a return to order and greatness and benefited from improved economic conditions brought about by an increase in the price of oil and other commodities. To maintain power, Putin's government has used the standard tricks of authoritarian governments: manipulation of elections, harassment of opponents (including occasional assassinations as well as imprisonment after rigged trials), censorship and intimidation of independent journalists, and limitations on political associations not connected with the government or Putin's party, United Russia. All of these activities violate human rights enshrined in the ECHR. But, as Human Rights Watch explains, "While Russia continues to pay the required monetary compensation to victims, it fails to meaningfully implement the core of the judgments by not conducting effective investigations, failing to hold perpetrators accountable, and using statutes of limitation and amnesties acts to avoid holding perpetrators to account."[9] Because the fines are small, they do not deter these activities.

Commentators have praised the Court for some aggressive rulings that took it beyond the text of the European Convention or risked offense to powerful countries. For example, in Dudgeon v. United Kingdom (1981), the Court barred criminalization of homosexual behavior; in Smith and Grady v. United Kingdom (1999), the Court found that discharge from the military based on homosexuality violated the right to a private life; in Mikheyev v. Russia (2006), the Court held that electric shocks used in police interrogations were torture and ordered Russia to pay compensation to the victim. The Court has also intervened in many other sensitive matters, restricting interrogation methods, detention practices, and regulations of press freedom.

Why don't countries agree to expand the Court, so that it can provide access to justice to more victims of human rights violations? The immediate answer is that for a number of years, Russia blocked efforts to expand the Court before finally giving way in 2010, when it agreed to give the Court new powers to dismiss frivolous claims. But Russia's opposition was a symptom of a larger problem: there is a limit to how much countries are willing to subject themselves to the jurisdiction of an international court. Although countries give the ECHR formal power to order them about, they limit its practical power by starving it of resources and limiting the remedies that it may award, and mediating its effects through the Council of Ministers, a political body that can take into account political constraints on the member states' ability or willingness to comply with judgments.

At the same time, where the ECHR has succeeded in causing reforms, it has provoked a backlash. In Hirst v. United Kingdom, the Court held that the United Kingdom had violated article 3 of Protocol 1 of the Convention by disenfranchising a prisoner serving time for manslaughter. The provision in question says "The High Contracting Parties undertake to hold free elections at reasonable intervals by secret ballot, under conditions which will ensure the free expression of the opinion of the people in the choice of the legislature." It says nothing about prisoners having the right to franchise, and, in 1952, the year that the Protocol was agreed to, it would not have occurred to anyone that prisoners might have a human right to vote. The ruling caused turmoil in the United Kingdom. People felt that the ECHR had imposed a rule on the country that it had never agreed to. But once one sets up an international court, one takes the risk that it will use its power in this way. In recent years, UK officials have ratcheted up threats to leave the European Convention because of their displeasure with some of the rulings.

2.4. INTERNATIONAL CRIMINAL LAW AND JUDICIAL INSTITUTIONS

There is a body of international law called international criminal law. It is different from human rights law but the impulses behind human rights law animate international criminal law as well. The common premise of the two bodies of law is that individuals should be protected from abuse at the hands of the state. International criminal law imposes liability on individuals, such as soldiers or leaders, while human rights law, as is typical for international law, is directed at states. Thus, a soldier violates international criminal law by killing a prisoner of war, while a state violates human rights law when its government orders that detainees be tortured. To be sure, we would also say that the state violates international law in the first case if it orders or authorizes the soldier to kill prisoners—but we do not normally say that the state has acted criminally. From this difference follows the remedy. If a soldier violates international criminal law, he can be tried and punished. If a state violates human rights law, whatever remedy that is available will be directed at the state—for example, under the European Convention it may be fined. A final and important difference is that international criminal law applies to a very narrow set of human rights violations, the very worst—killing, torture, and the like. A government official would not violate international criminal law by depriving citizens of their human rights to vote, engage in free expression, or be protected from discrimination on the basis of sex.

International criminal law predates human rights law by centuries. In the eighteenth century, countries regarded piracy and certain violations of the law of war as international crimes. The fact that these were international crimes meant that the normal rule in international law that countries are responsible for prosecuting people for crimes committed on their own territory was suspended, and any country could prosecute anyone for committing international crimes, regardless of the location of the crime and regardless of the nationalities of the defendant or victim. This was especially important for piracy because no country had jurisdiction over the high seas, and pirates could otherwise avoid jurisdiction by flying the flag of a country unlikely to prosecute them (or no flag at all).

But like human rights law, international criminal law became a major force in international law only in the second half of the twentieth century. The parallel does not end here. There was an initial burst of enthusiasm for international criminal law at the end of World War II, when international trials were held at Nuremberg and Tokyo. The Allies argued that German and Japanese leaders violated the laws of war as well as committed "crimes against peace" and "crimes against humanity," and tried them, executing several. At the same time, the Universal Declaration was being negotiated. However, it wasn't long before the Cold War threw international criminal law into a deep freeze, just as it did for human rights law.

International criminal law flowered in the 1990s. A civil war broke out in the Balkans, and various armies and paramilitary units committed numerous atrocities against civilians, including what came to be known as "ethnic cleansing"—the deliberate attempt by one ethnic or national group to expel members of minority groups from the territory on which they all lived. The Security Council established an International Tribunal for the Former Yugoslavia, and gave it jurisdiction over the international crimes committed in that area. Then in 1994, a genocide took place in Rwanda, and the Security Council established a second tribunal to try participants in the genocide. At the end of the decade, countries negotiated a new tribunal known as the International Criminal Court, which was given jurisdiction over international crimes committed on the territory of its members or by their nationals. The ICC has been in operation for more than a decade.

The quality of the performance of these tribunals has been hotly contested. Both the Yugoslavia and Rwanda tribunals convicted major international criminals, but not very many of them, and at immense cost over a very long period of time. As of July 2013, the Yugoslavia tribunal had indicted 161 persons, concluded proceedings for 115, and sentenced 56, and its trials on average lasted about a year. The Tribunal's two-year budget for operating in 2012 and 2013 was $250,814,000. As of February 2013, the Rwanda tribunal had indicted 93 people and completed 75 cases. Of those, they had convicted 47. The budget for the Rwanda Tribunal was $174,320,000 for 2012 and 2013 (down from $257,080,000 in 2010 and 2011). In other words, the two tribunals spent several billion dollars over almost 20 years to convict less than half a dozen people per year on average, a tiny fraction of the thousands of perpetrators.

The ICC has also experienced growing pains. As of July 2013, the ICC had opened eight investigations, indicted 30 people, and heard or begun hearing only 18 cases. Only a few cases have reached the end of their proceeding; the ICC has obtained one conviction; one case ended in an acquittal, and seven cases were dismissed. Of the eight open investigations, all are of African countries: the Democratic Republic of the Congo, the Central African Republic, Uganda, Sudan, Kenya, Libya, Côte d'Ivoire, and Mali. All 18 of the cases before the ICC involve African defendants. The focus on Africa, while understandable in light of that continent's immense problems, and in many cases resulting from requests of the countries involved, has nonetheless produced accusations of bias, and threats by African countries to withdraw from the ICC unless it accommodates their interests.

This book concerns human rights law, not international criminal law, but it is worth pausing to note a parallel between experiences with the two bodies of law. International criminal law is generally thought to block the worst of atrocities. Thus, a starting point for international criminal law is genocide, where an entire population is wiped out. But line-drawing problems quickly intrude. The settings in which international crimes are committed—usually messy insurgencies and civil wars—typically involve thousands of people acting in different groups, who use different tactics and have different aims even when they are (sometimes temporarily) on the same side. Hence, the paramilitary that enters a village to wipe out the Muslims may have various complicated relationships with other groups, who will be accused of complicity in genocide. And people with genocidal intent often end up killing very few victims because they meet opposition or are poorly organized, while other groups without genocidal intent may kill a huge amount of people. The first group nonetheless commits genocide or attempted genocide under international law, while the second group may be swept under the catch-all "crimes against humanity," which includes murder, enslavement, deportation, torture, sexual violence, "persecution" on racial or other group-based grounds, enforced disappearances, apartheid, and "other inhumane acts," as long as part of a "widespread or systematic attack" against a civilian population; or, if not, "war crimes," which includes an even more general list of violations, involving "wilfully causing great suffering" and "committing outrages upon personal dignity"—or complicity in any of these things, which expands the set of potential criminal defendants by orders of magnitude.

In every war and civil conflict—of which there are dozens at any one time—all of these crimes are being committed. Logistics alone make it impossible to try everyone who has committed one of these crimes, especially if the trial is to be fair. Political considerations will also necessarily loom large: as the Allies learned after World War II, often people who are complicit in serious crimes are needed to run the country if it is ever to be reconstructed and peaceful relations reestablished. Often peace is possible only if law-violators on both sides of a conflict receive amnesties. Thus, if trials are to be held, the defendants must be carefully chosen, with the three chief considerations being how serious the offense, how easy it is to convict, and how important the defendant is for political rapprochement of warring groups. Because it is usually easiest to convict various low-level officials like police and foot soldiers who fail to hide their tracks and actually pulled the triggers rather than issued veiled orders, the temptation is always to go after these less important perpetrators until complaints that the major wrongdoers have escaped justice become overwhelming. The criminal law had to be expanded—a hypertrophy that parallels the hypertrophy of human rights law—in order to ensure that those at the top could be convicted (usually on complicity-related grounds). But as a result, prosecuting authorities, usually acting on behalf of foreign states or (as in the case of the ICC) on their own, have broad discretion to choose who to try and who not to try.

Thanks to the central role of courts in international criminal law, which can maintain a kind of jurisprudential order by issuing opinions that accompany concrete punishments or acquittals, the content of international criminal law is not as amorphous as international human rights law, although its actual impact on the conduct of governments is just as unclear. But the practicalities and limitations of enforcement in the context of mass atrocities entail that prosecutors be given immense discretion to choose who will be prosecuted.

Because there is no "neutral" way to exercise that discretion, states have been extremely reluctant to subject themselves to international criminal courts, and have gone to great lengths to limit their powers, just as they have done for human rights bodies.

2.5. NATIONAL INSTITUTIONS

When states enter into treaties, they typically must implement them by issuing orders to domestic institutions. In many nations, the treaties automatically become judicially enforceable or administratively enforced domestic law; in other nations, additional legislation must be enacted that makes the treaty obligations enforceable as domestic law. When treaties merely confirm existing domestic law, no action is necessary.

The domestic enforcement of human rights treaties initially followed this pattern. Many liberal democracies entered into human rights treaties with the expectation that they would not need to take any action because the rights in those treaties were already rights that people enjoyed under domestic law. Other states passed new laws or revised their constitutions, or governments issued administrative orders to soldiers and civil servants. The most significant development is that in certain democracies—notably, Australia—human rights treaties provided a basis for judicial enforcement of rights that were normally incorporated by statute.

Human rights treaties also gave rise to an unusual development: the proliferation of National Human Rights Institutions, as they are known in UN jargon. These are domestic institutions that governments have created that have a specific mission of promoting and protecting human rights, acting outside courts and existing bureaucratic structures. These NHRIs—they are typically called human rights commissions or ombudsmen—come in a bewildering variety of forms, but all possess some combination of powers to educate people about human rights, investigate complaints about human rights violations, issue (non-binding) judgments about alleged violations, and make recommendations for reform. Little is known as to how effectively they function. No doubt there is considerable variation in their effectiveness across countries.

CHAPTER THREE

Why Do States Enter into Human Rights Treaties?

3.1. TO IMPROVE HUMAN RIGHTS

Normally, when states negotiate treaties, it is easy to identify the gains they expect to obtain. For instance, let's take two states that enter into a trade treaty requiring each state to reduce its tariffs on goods exported from the other. The states enter into the treaty because the gains from trade (profits for their exporters, cheap imported goods for consumers) exceed the losses (lost profits for domestic industries that compete with imports). The states comply with the treaty as long as the benefits exceed the costs, and as long as each state fears that if it violates the treaty, the other state will retaliate by doing the same.

It is not clear that a similar story explains why states ratify human rights treaties. To see why, consider three groups of states: liberal democracies, authoritarian countries, and transitional countries.

When liberal democracies ratify human rights treaties, they typically do not expect to change their own behavior (but see section 3.2, below, for another view). They often take the lead in drafting the human rights treaties, and these treaties typically track the rights that the liberal democracies already respect.

This is confirmed by what has happened when liberal democracies disagreed over whether certain rights should be regarded as human rights. One such disagreement concerned the death penalty. Many democracies reject the death penalty, but others, including the United States and India, do not. The countries therefore agreed to incorporate a ban on the death penalty into an Optional Protocol, and the countries that rejected the ban declined to ratify that protocol. Thus, there was no sense that liberal democracies must reach a consensus or that one group must fall in line with the position of the other. In other cases, the countries would ratify a treaty but add a reservation in which they state that they would not comply with one or more provisions that they disagreed with—for example, as we saw above, the requirement that adult and juvenile prisoners be segregated.

But while liberal democracies do not expect to change their behavior, they clearly expect other countries—repressive countries like China, for example—to change *their* behavior and start respecting human rights. Why would democracies care about how foreign governments treat their foreign populations? One possible reason is that people in liberal democracies are altruistic, and care about the well-being of people in foreign countries. This hypothesis is supported by some evidence: people make donations to help victims of famines in foreign countries, and support (albeit often grudgingly) foreign aid programs. Anecdotal evidence suggests people in the West feel real, though often transitory, distress when they learn about atrocities taking place in foreign countries.

A second hypothesis is that democracies believe that the type of government that abuses human rights is also the type of government that is likely to cause war. As we saw in Chapter 1, section 1.2, this was one lesson drawn from Nazism. And common experience does suggest that many of the worst rights-abusing countries are sources of instability—Iraq under Saddam Hussein, for example, or Cuba, or North Korea. They quarrel with their neighbors, drive refugees into foreign countries, export revolution, battle with insurgents who cross borders in order to regroup, shelter terrorists, and collapse into civil war. Survey evidence also suggests that Americans believe that countries that violate human rights are more likely to pose a threat to American interests than are countries that respect human rights, and are therefore a more appropriate target for military intervention.

Thus, as a starting point, one can posit that liberal democracies enter into human rights treaties because those treaties impose no costs on those states while requiring authoritarian states to adopt liberal values, which should both improve the well-being of people living in authoritarian states and promote international stability.

This raises the question, however, of why authoritarian countries would ratify human rights treaties. It seems that authoritarian governments would gain nothing from entering into such treaties because, as we saw, democracies do not change their behavior, and even if they did, it is hard to believe that an authoritarian government that abuses the human rights of its own population would see any gain from entering into a treaty that causes liberal democracies to improve their own human rights conduct. So, again, the model of the trade treaty, where both sides obtain reciprocal benefits, is inapt.

There are several possible reasons why authoritarian states enter into human rights treaties. Many of these countries are poor countries and depend on the West for foreign aid, technical assistance, defense, and other benefits. Thus, when Western countries press them to ratify human rights treaties, they cannot afford to say no. At the same time, the governments of these countries do not expect that the human rights treaties will actually compel them to improve their treatment of their populations. Domestic courts will not enforce them, either because they lack the authority under domestic constitutional arrangements, or because they lack independence from the government. And dictators do not expect Western countries to pressure them to comply with the treaties for reasons that I will discuss in Chapter 5. Ultimately, they ratify the treaties because they do not want to offend Western countries, but also do not expect to incur any costs from doing so. However, a recent paper found no evidence that nations that ratify human rights treaties receive foreign aid as a reward or even that they are showered with praise from Western countries.[1]

Authoritarian countries that are not poor or dependent on the West might see human rights treaties from a public relations vantage, as a way of reassuring their own citizens or foreigners that they care about human rights. As I discussed in Chapter 1, the Soviet Union initially championed the ICESCR because it embodied the Soviet vision of economic rights. Countries felt compelled to ratify the Convention on Torture because torture is unpopular. The treaties provided a vehicle for states to announce that they supported the values they believed the relevant audience, whether domestic or foreign, cared about. But it is one thing to announce one's support for values, and another to actually support them.

Transitional states provide another case. The transitional state is a state that is undergoing a changeover from an authoritarian system to democracy. Important examples include the eastern European states after 1989, southern European countries in the 1970s, Latin American countries in the 1980s, and South Korea. Andrew Moravcsik argues that the governments of these countries enter into human rights treaties in order to lock in liberal reforms.[2] A government might worry that liberal rights could be abandoned whenever a liberal government is replaced by an authoritarian government supported by people nostalgic for old times. By ratifying human rights treaties, the liberal government would make it more difficult for future governments to do this sort of thing. It may be difficult or embarrassing to withdraw from a treaty, and violation of the treaty could give rise to international pressure.

A case in point is Hungary, which ratified the European Convention on Human Rights in 1992, just as it was undergoing a transition to democracy. In recent years, the government has moved to the right, and has begun taking actions that are inconsistent with the ECHR— such as reducing the independence of the judiciary, restricting religious freedom, and curbing certain political freedoms. European authorities have put pressure on Hungary to reverse these moves, but it is too soon to know whether these efforts will be successful.

Putting all of these motivations together, the story goes like this. Liberal democracies entered into human rights treaties mainly to pressure authoritarian countries and perhaps help transitional countries—with the goal, based on both altruistic and strategic considerations, of improving respect for human rights around the world. Authoritarian countries entered into these treaties in response to external pressure, or for reasons of internal (or external) propaganda, but did not expect to comply with them. Transitional countries entered into these treaties mainly based on internal considerations, in the hope of locking in liberal reforms.

One can see some inconsistencies here. The authoritarian countries entered into the treaties because they believed they would not be enforced, while the democracies and transitional countries entered into them because they believed they would be enforced. How could sophisticated governments have had such conflicting views? I will return to this puzzle in Chapter 5.

3.2. THE COSTS OF ENTERING INTO HUMAN RIGHTS TREATIES

I said above that liberal democracies do not expect to incur any costs from entering into human rights treaties, in the sense of being forced by the treaties to engage in behavior that they would not otherwise be inclined to engage in. But if this were true, one would expect all democracies to enter into these treaties, at least if the benefit is greater than zero. Yet not all democracies do—above all, the United States, which has refused to ratify the ICESCR and the CRC, among others. Why not?

One answer is that some liberal states do not ratify human rights treaties because they face legislative or constitutional hurdles, and judicial constraints—all of which raise the domestic costs of ratification. The United States, for example, normally may ratify a treaty only if two thirds of the Senate provide consent. This means that a minority of senators with outlier ideologies can block a treaty for no good reason. Most democracies, however, do not have such a high threshold for entering into a treaty, and even in the United States, the question remains why outlier senators would block a treaty that is costless. After all, the United States has ratified thousands of treaties—many more than any other country.

A more significant problem for liberal democracies is that independent judiciaries may interpret treaties in a way contrary to the intentions of the government. The United States government took this problem seriously enough to insist on adding declarations to human rights treaties that said that the treaties are not domestically enforceable. Even this might not be enough, however, as, in various, often unpredictable ways, human rights treaties have in fact influenced U.S. judges. In some cases, they have been used to resolve ambiguities in statutes and even in the U.S. Constitution; in other cases, they have been used in tort litigation against human rights violators by means of a statute that authorizes plaintiffs to bring tort suits that violate international law. Embarrassments can occur when state governments refuse to comply with human rights treaties and the national government finds itself unable to compel them. But taking all of these things together, they are pretty trivial, and it would be surprising if they really explained why the United States has entered into fewer human rights treaties than other democracies. Similarly, it seems unlikely that these costs are high for other liberal democracies.

Non-democracies and democracies with weak human rights records face different incentives. If they expect the human rights treaties to have coercive effect—either by inspiring domestic pressure or facilitating foreign pressure—then entering into the treaties is costly, in the sense that it will require them to change behavior in ways they are not inclined to do. On the other hand, the governments of these countries might expect instead that (1) ratification will actually reduce foreign pressure because foreign countries will accept it as a good-faith accommodation; (2) ratification makes no difference because foreign countries and domestic interests will pressure them to improve human rights regardless of whether they ratify human rights treaties or not; (3) ratification does not empower domestic human rights groups because they are politically weak or cannot take advantage of domestic legal institutions; (4) foreign countries are just not as concerned about human rights performance as other matters such as trade and security; or (5) they will always be able to claim that they are in compliance with the human rights treaties because the obligations are vague and conflicting, or—in some cases—too demanding to be realistically imposed on countries with weak institutions. For all these reasons, ratification of a human rights treaty may seem like a costless propaganda exercise.

A few authors have attempted to determine statistically why some states enter into human rights treaties while others do not. The results suggest that democratic states that commit few human rights violations are more likely to enter into these treaties than are democratic states that commit many human rights violations, or non-democratic states. Newer states are also more likely to enter into human rights treaties than are older states; and regional pressure plays a role. Human rights treaty ratification is also correlated with democracy, Protestant-religion domination, left-wing government at the time of ratification, and legal institutions that make it easier to enter into treaties. Common-law countries are less likely to ratify human rights treaties than countries with other legal systems.[3] But given that nearly all countries have ratified nearly all the human rights treaties over a relatively compressed period—differing mainly in how long it had taken them to do so—one must doubt that the specific characteristics of states play a significant role in determining why they enter into human rights treaties. A more plausible hypothesis is that, for most countries, once a human rights treaty is put on the agenda, it becomes hard to resist the pressure to ratify it because of the symbolic importance of looking like a good global citizen and the absence of practical consequences from being in violation of the treaty.

3.3. THE "WESTERN IMPERIALISM" CRITICISM AND ITS LIMITS

An old criticism of international human rights law is that it is a kind of imperialism, an effort by the West to exert control over its former colonies. Commentators who hold this view point out that even during the heyday of nineteenth-century imperialism, the imperialist powers often conceived of themselves as having a "civilizing mission," which allowed them to rationalize their domination of foreign populations. The ideology of this civilizing mission resembles some of the thinking behind the modern human rights regime. The British were fond of saying that the conquered natives lacked a sense of rights—rights to liberty and property—and thus could not govern themselves in an enlightened way. In the eyes of the critics, the human rights regime is tainted by this association, and perhaps is just a new way for Western powers to control nominally independent states.

The argument should not be dismissed out of hand; it is easy to think of ways that human rights, or at least certain human rights, could be used to advance Western interests or protect earlier gains. During the era of decolonization, roughly from the 1940s to the 1960s, Western governments relaxed their hold on their colonies, but they usually maintained economic contacts. Western corporations held massive property interests in those countries, including ownership interests in mines or farmland. The newly liberated populations would learn that they were not permitted to expropriate these property interests because international law forbade them from doing so. But that meant, in the eyes of those populations, that the former colonizers would not be forced to return property that they had stolen in the first place.

Moreover, modern human rights debates bear a noticeable resemblance to human rights controversies in the past. British imperial administrators in colonial India were disgusted and horrified by suttee (the practice of burning alive the wives of deceased husbands) and eventually banned it, but only after much hesitation because the ban contradicted the standing policy of tolerating local religious customs. The Indians themselves were ambivalent about suttee and some of them welcomed the ban while others opposed it. Much like modern defenders of human rights, anti-imperialist critics of suttee argued that indigenous cultural norms provided the resources for criticizing suttee, and so the custom should not be celebrated by anti-imperialists just because the British opposed it. The resemblance to modern debates over female genital cutting—a ritual practice in many African countries—is hard to ignore.

At one time, the criticism of human rights as a form of Western imperialism enjoyed numerous adherents, and was advanced by Western academics and leaders of developing countries alike. Today, however, it holds less sway, and it is easy to see why. First, it implies that countries in Africa, Latin America, and Asia would be better off if they reverted to pre-colonial forms of rule, which of course were hardly democratic, and featured torture and other unsavory practices. Second, commentators have pointed out that many non-Western countries have traditions that are compatible with modern human rights—for example, the simple idea that people are equal. Although these traditions did not predominate as they did in the West, and were often advanced by individuals or groups who did poorly under dominant political and social norms, their existence contradicts the notion that human rights is a wholly foreign imposition. Third, the most prominent proponents of these arguments were dictators and their lackeys—and who wants to be associated with them?

Still, the suspicion that modern human rights is an updated version of the civilizing mission of Western imperialists is hard to shake and should make one uneasy, as it implies either that modern human rights thinking suffers from a serious moral taint or that the civilizing mission of the imperialists—who introduced literacy and other rudimentary forms of education, modern health care, legal institutions, and other goods that are today guaranteed by human rights law—has received more opprobrium than is justified. Defenders of human rights must probably grasp the second horn of this dilemma. I prefer the first. A less aggressive version of this argument, which I will return to later in this book, is that modern human rights thinking is not so much a mask for imperialist designs or a way to exert power over vulnerable populations, as it is a symptom of a weakness in humanitarian thinking that the civilizing impulse of the nineteenth century shared: a hubristic sense that we know better than people in foreign countries how to improve their lives, accompanied by sloppy mental habits that make it difficult to distinguish our interests from theirs.

CHAPTER FOUR

Do States Comply with Human Rights Treaties?

4.1. HUMAN RIGHTS TREATIES AND THE QUESTION OF COMPLIANCE

Until recently, there was little discussion in the academic literature about whether human rights treaties cause countries to respect human rights. Oddly, two different groups of academics and commentators made opposite assumptions. International lawyers and human rights advocates assumed that human rights treaties did cause countries to improve their treatment of their citizens. After all, a lot of diplomatic effort was put into negotiating these treaties, encouraging or coercing countries to ratify them, and then complaining when countries violated their treaty obligations. Numerous NGOs devoted themselves to the cause of human rights. Powerful countries imposed sanctions on human rights violators like South Africa during the era of Apartheid, and even used military force against them—for example, NATO's military interventions during the Balkan wars of the 1990s or the U.S.-led invasion of Iraq in 2003.

Some Western governments make aid conditional on compliance, or at least improved compliance, with human rights norms.

Another group of academics, mainly political scientists, assumed that human rights treaties did *not* have any effect on the behavior of countries; indeed, these academics, who typically called themselves "realists," assumed that international law generally did not affect the behavior of states. They saw the international arena as a security competition among different states, a zero-sum game in which one state's gain was another state's loss. In such conditions, states could gain little by cooperating with each other—except in temporary military alliances or security agreements that could fall apart at a moment's notice. International law could play a minimal role or none at all, was perhaps just an illusion, a sophisticated kind of propaganda—a set of rules that would be swept away whenever the balance of power changed.

The first view is too optimistic, the second too skeptical. Closer examination of the behavior of governments presents a mixed picture. It is easy to find examples where countries enter into human rights treaties and change their behavior. The political scientist Beth Simmons describes how Japan and Colombia ratified CEDAW, and then afterward either passed legislation or constitutional amendments that implemented its provisions or were compelled by their own courts to respect CEDAW's provisions.[1] In Simmons's account, it is not entirely clear why the countries ratified the treaties. But once the treaties were ratified, they had an observable impact on political activity. Women's rights groups cited the treaty in the course of advocating legislation, and litigants cited the treaty in their complaints against employers that treated them unequally and governments that denied them reproductive rights. In Japan, the legislation passed in response to CEDAW was weak (it did not provide for penalties for discrimination) but it seems to have modestly improved equality in salaries and college enrollment, among other things. In Colombia, the government improved health services for women and access to contraception, while the courts took some steps toward liberalizing its strict law against abortion.

The puzzle is how to reconcile accounts like this one with the many examples of blatant human rights violations. As we have discussed already, many parties to the ICCPR, including Vietnam and Uzbekistan, have authoritarian political regimes with few political freedoms. Saudi Arabia ratified the treaty banning discrimination against women in 2007, and yet by law subordinates women to men in all areas of life. Child labor exists in countries that have ratified the treaty on the rights of the child—Uzbekistan, Tanzania, and India, for example. Powerful Western countries, including the United States, do business with grave human rights abusers to which they offer economic benefits or diplomatic support. South Africa during the Apartheid era aside, it is hard to identify concerted efforts by major nations, acting independently or collectively, to pressure human rights violators to improve their behavior on the basis of human rights violations, as opposed to security concerns of the sort posed by Iran and North Korea.

In recent years, Western efforts to impose sanctions on Sudan caused that country to strengthen its ties with China. The Arab Spring, which initially seemed like a great flowering of human rights, has collapsed—with an authoritarian regime taking over Egypt, and a brutal civil war in Syria. Western countries did not encourage pro-democracy groups at the outset of the Arab Spring, partly because they feared the chaos that would accompany the collapse of authoritarian regimes. International organizations have not filled the vacuum either because they are controlled by Western powers or are too weak to act against them.

The methodological problems with trying to show the effect of human rights treaties are formidable. It is tempting to assume that if a government ratifies a human rights treaty and then passes a law that implements that treaty, the treaty has had the desired effect. The problem is that many countries do not enforce their laws, or their laws are too weak to affect people's behavior. If a country passes a law against torture after ratifying the CAT, but then immunizes its security services, then the treaty has not had an effect. If the law does not formally create immunity, but no prosecutions are brought under it, then it has also had no effect. Laws that improve judicial procedure and give greater protections to defendants might cause police to use extra-judicial methods—torture, harassment, killings—to maintain order, so while human rights improvements will be seen in one area, the net effect may be nil or even negative. Similarly, a law that provides greater health services to women—as described by Simmons—might result in fewer funds for schools, so that the net effect of the law is to improve compliance with CEDAW but reduce compliance with the ICESCR. Moreover, the data for most countries is sparse, so it is very hard to know what countries do in the first place.

Starting about 10 years ago, scholars began to address these questions systematically by using statistical data to evaluate the performance of human rights treaties. Their studies are the subject of the next two sections.

4.2. SOME DATA

The statistical studies try to measure the effect of human rights treaties in a rigorous way. They put aside anecdotes, which can mislead, and focus on data. The design of these studies is straightforward. Researchers seek to determine whether a human rights treaty affects a state's treatment of its population in the manner that the treaty dictates. The Convention Against Torture should reduce torture. Thus, for every state, one examines the state's treatment of the population before it enters into the treaty and after it enters into the treaty. If the Convention Against Torture has a causal effect, then a state's use of torture should decline after it ratifies the treaty (or possibly even before ratification if the government takes steps to reduce torture in anticipation of its future legal obligation to do so)—and the decline should be meaningful rather than trivial.

This approach greatly improves on anecdotal evidence, but it is easy to abuse or misunderstand. No statistical technique can completely rule out spurious correlations, so studies that appear to show that treaty ratification improves human rights performance must be evaluated with care.

Let us begin by looking at the relationship between the number of countries that have ratified the ICCPR over time and the political rights that they grant to their populations, as measured by Freedom House. In Figure 4.1, below, the solid line shows the number of ICCPR member states; the broken line shows the average political rights score (1 is worst, 7 is best).

The ICCPR was signed in 1966 and became effective in 1976. In the intervening years a few dozen states ratified it; the number would increase to almost 170 by 2012. The solid line in Figure 4.1 shows that the number of countries that have ratified the ICCPR has increased steadily. Meanwhile, the average global political rights score increased from 2.61 to 3.65.

Does Figure 4.1 suggest that the ICCPR caused states to improve human rights? Certainly, there is a positive relationship, but it looks weak, and other explanations are possible—for example, the increasing wealth of the world or greater trade—accounting both for the improvement in scores and the increase in ratifications. Since the early 1990s, 40 countries ratified the ICCPR but average scores hardly budged.

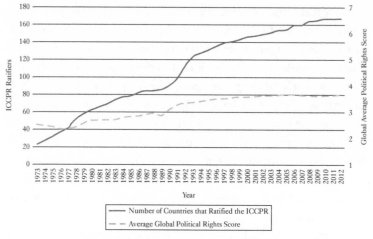

Figure 4.1 ICCPR and Civil Liberties
Note: Freedom House's scores have been reversed (so 1 is worst rather than best). *Source*: Freedom House, http://www.freedomhouse.org/.

We might also ask whether the state behavior Freedom House looks at is the same as the state behavior required by the ICCPR. The ICCPR obviously does not direct states to improve "political rights" in the sense defined by Freedom House, so to measure its effectiveness, a more useful approach is to match individual provisions with the corresponding activities of the states. Figure 4.2, below, provides this information for the CAT, which outlaws torture.

The x-axis shows the five years before and after a country ratified the CAT. Year 0 is the year that the country ratified the CAT. For example, year 0 for the United States was 1994, while year 0 for Nicaragua was 2005. The line shows the average torture score for countries during the five years leading up to ratification and the five years following ratification (where 0 refers to frequent torture

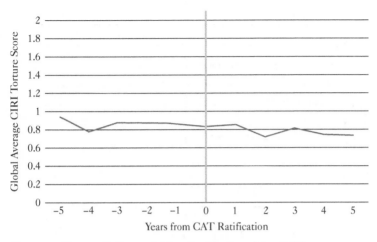

Figure 4.2 Torture Before and After Ratification of the CAT

and 2 refers to no torture). If the average country had reduced torture during this period, then the line would have sloped up. In fact, it slopes down slightly—suggesting that the amount of torture increased during this period.

In Figure 4.3, we look at the ICCPR and four types of human rights violations—violations of freedom of speech, extrajudicial killings, violations of freedom of religion, and infringements on the independence of the judiciary.

There is some improvement in the year before the treaty was ratified for all four measures, but most of the gains erode over the following years for freedom of speech and extrajudicial killings. But even for freedom of religion and freedom of judiciary, improvement has been minimal, and it is ambiguous whether the improvements took place in anticipation of and because of treaty ratification or treaty ratification simply accompanied other trends that were already taking place.

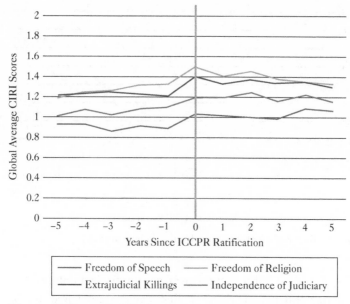

Figure 4.3 Effects of ICCPR on Four Types of Political Rights

4.3. THE STUDIES

These graphs should give pause to people who have assumed that the spread of human rights law has improved people's well-being by leading to real protection of their rights. A wave of statistical studies has confirmed the negative impression, albeit with some minor qualifications. Some evidence suggests that certain authoritarian regimes actually engaged in more violations after ratifying human rights treaties; other evidence suggests that certain subcategories of state—such as democratic states with strong NGOs—improved their performance after ratifying human rights treaties. There is also evidence that states that enter into human rights treaties incorporate some of those rights into their national constitutions,[2] although many of those countries do not in fact respect the rights in their own constitutions.[3] Also, some interesting but hard-to-interpret evidence suggests that the existence of human rights has penetrated public consciousness in some countries,[4] and that the public may believe that the government should comply with the treaties it has ratified.[5] The overall picture at the aggregate level, however, is that human rights treaties do not systematically improve human rights outcomes.[6]

A book by Beth Simmons paints a somewhat rosier picture. Simmons examined the effects of 13 treaties or treaty provisions. In six cases, the results did not achieve statistical significance. In line with previous research, Simmons found that countries that ratified the CAT did not stop torturing people, for example. In seven cases, an improvement in human rights was associated with ratification of a relevant treaty. Countries that ratified an optional protocol of the ICCPR that bans the death penalty did in fact ban the death penalty. In countries that ratified CEDAW, the ratio of girls to boys in schools increased by 5.5 percent, relative to countries that did not ratify CEDAW; governments self-reported that they were more likely to provide women with access to birth control, although the magnitude of the effect is difficult to interpret; and the employment of women by the government improved by almost 3 percent. Finally, in countries that ratified the Convention on the Rights of the Child, the rate of child labor decreased and the rate of child immunization increased. In another study, Yonatan Lupu finds, consistent with other studies, that countries that ratify the ICCPR and the CAT do not have better records with respect to political rights and torture than other countries, but also finds that countries that ratify CEDAW do improve their respect for the political, economic, and social rights of women.[7]

The studies also suggest that treaty ratification improves human rights in certain types of countries rather than in all countries.

Freedom of religion, for instance, progresses more in countries undergoing a democratic transition than in other countries. And while the average country that ratifies the ICCPR does not improve fair trial practices, transitional countries (countries that are undergoing a transition from an authoritarian system to a democratic system) do. Transitional countries, unlike the average country, also reduce torture after ratifying the CAT. Other types of slicing and dicing of data—regarding, for example, the income of a country or its religiosity—yields evidence that certain types of countries may be more responsive to treaty ratification than are other types.

Understood in the best possible light,[8] these studies suggest that a small number of treaty provisions may have improved a small number of human rights outcomes in a small number of countries by a small, possibly trivial amount. They do not show that the treaties improved the overall well-being of people in those countries because it is unknown whether governments complied with treaty obligations by taking resources away from other projects that served the public interest or shifted resources from more visible to less visible means of repression. Realistically, one can have little confidence that the treaties have improved people's lives.

CHAPTER FIVE

Why Do States Comply (or Not Comply) with Human Rights Treaties?

5.1. INTERNATIONAL INCENTIVES TO COMPLY

In the case of ordinary treaties, the main reason that states comply with their obligations is that they fear that if they do not, other treaty parties will violate their own obligations. As we have seen, this logic does not easily carry over to human rights treaties. If Sweden and Guatemala enter into the Convention Against Torture, and Guatemala then tortures political prisoners, Sweden is not likely to retaliate by torturing its own citizens. It is possible that Sweden and other parties to the Convention Against Torture will take action against Guatemala, in order to compel it to bring its conduct in alignment with the treaty. For example, they could threaten to cut off foreign aid (if they supply foreign aid), or offer foreign aid conditional on improvements in human rights, threaten to withdraw support for diplomatic initiatives favored by Guatemala, drag their feet on an extradition, reduce the number of visas offered to Guatemalans who seek work, and so on.

But it is not so easy. Most countries do not have significant relations with Guatemala, and so have no leverage against it. If Sweden does not give foreign aid to Guatemala, or gives it only a little, then it cannot make a credible threat to withhold aid if Guatemala violates human rights. Indeed, Sweden might feel that if it does withhold whatever foreign aid it gives Guatemala, poor people will suffer, and the government will not be deterred—so it is unlikely to withdraw the aid even in response to serious government wrongdoing. Guatemala's neighbors might have some leverage, as they and Guatemala share interests over migration, fishing rights, and so on, but those neighbors need Guatemala as much as Guatemala needs them. If they threaten non-cooperation over, say, migration, then they hurt themselves. Perhaps, if Guatemala's trade partners banded together and refused to trade with it unless it improved human rights, that would have an effect. But most of a country's trade partners will be its neighbors, who will have the same sorts of problems. In addition, cutting off a country from trade risks impoverishing its population further. And these countries have their own human rights problems, so any complaint about Guatemala's will lack credibility.

Powerful countries like the United States can exert pressure effectively because so many countries rely on them for trade, security, technological assistance, and other benefits. But powerful countries also care about maintaining geopolitical peace. The United States has tolerated human rights violations in many of its strategic allies—pro-Western dictatorships during the Cold War, and most big and strategically important countries today. Other human rights-violating countries like Russia and China (and the United States itself when it used torture in the years after 9/11) are immune to economic pressure.

Even powerful countries often cannot exert sufficient pressure on a human rights violator to cause it to improve its behavior, because the target of sanctions can often retaliate by improving its ties with the sanctioning countries' rivals. Western efforts to isolate Sudan, for example, failed because Sudan strengthened its economic relationship with China, to which it sold oil. During the Cold War, the United States tolerated human rights abuses in pro-Western countries in the developing world in part because it believed that if it pressured those countries, they would switch allegiance to the Soviet side.

Moreover, even when all states care about human rights violations in a particular state, they face a collective action problem. Although every state may want to end the human rights violations, each state has a strong incentive to free ride, hoping that other states will incur the costs of sanctioning the country in question. This problem of collective action undermines efforts to create effective, independent institutions that enforce human rights. In the absence of a world government, states can cooperate only in decentralized fashion.

The evidence suggests that countries do not consistently cut aid to human rights violators, or otherwise put pressure on them. One study finds evidence that multinational institutions like the World Bank withdraw aid from or stop making loans to countries condemned by the UN Commission on Human Rights (now the UN Council on Human Rights), but the UN Commission did not consistently condemn the worst countries, so this pressure would be uneven at best.

From time to time, a country may be internationally isolated because of its human rights violations. South Africa is the most famous example. Countries isolated it because of its apartheid system, although not because South Africa violated any human rights treaties, as it carefully refrained from entering into them. South Africa officially abolished apartheid in 1990 and held multiracial elections in 1994, which brought to power a government supported by the black majority. At the same time, South Africa signed and then ratified the core human rights treaties.

Human rights violations also helped inspire support for NATO's intervention in the Balkans during the 1990s. But the intervention was driven mainly by strategic imperatives—NATO members feared refugee flows and other sources of disruption in Europe—as illustrated by the failure to intercede in Rwanda in 1994 during a significantly worse genocide that could have been stopped with fewer military resources. Economic sanctions and military force are generally not used against human rights violators unless they also pose a threat to other countries—North Korea is an example.

Some commentators argue that NGOs are the major source of pressure to comply with human rights treaties. They argue that NGOs like Human Rights Watch and Amnesty International collect funds from people who care about human rights, and then monitor countries and put public pressure on those that violate human rights. NGOs also provide technical assistance to governments that do not understand the treaties, or do not know how to implement them, including, for example, training programs for police and other government officials. NGOs do not face the strategic constraints of large states. Unlike elected officials in democracies, they are free of the pressures of fickle voters and greedy interest groups. And because they are able to gain the attention of the media, they can embarrass repressive governments and force them to improve their compliance with human rights treaties.

But this argument does not survive scrutiny. Because NGOs lack the power to coerce, they ultimately depend on their ability to persuade governments, voters, businesses, and other people and institutions to take action against those whom the NGOs identify as human rights violators. Occasionally, boycotts and other forms of pressure follow from those efforts, but their overall effectiveness is clearly limited.

5.2. DOMESTIC INCENTIVES TO COMPLY

Scholars have argued that states comply with international treaties because of domestic political pressures. One view is that voters (in democracies) or otherwise influential people (in non-democracies) pressure government officials to comply with human rights law. Another view is that interest groups or domestic NGOs pressure elected officials to comply with human rights law.

These arguments have some superficial plausibility. If domestic support exists for ratification of the human rights treaty, then one would think that domestic support would exist for compliance as well. But there is a certain oddness to the argument that domestic pressure or mobilization explains states' compliance with human rights treaties. If domestic pressure can force a government to respect human rights, then it will do so regardless of whether the government enters into a human rights treaty. If it cannot, then it will fail to do so even if the government enters into a human rights treaty. Normally, domestic political pressure causes a government to act (or fails to cause the government act) through domestic political institutions—electoral institutions, or law, or some such thing. If it succeeds in doing this, what does a treaty add?

There are several possible answers. One is that foreign (usually Western) countries put human rights on the domestic agenda by compelling a government to ratify a human rights treaty. This argument has been made about the Helsinki Accords. In the early 1970s the United States, the European countries, and the Soviet Union sought to stabilize their relationship. To this end, they entered into an agreement under which the West recognized the Soviet Union's sphere of influence over Eastern Europe, and the Soviet Union and the Eastern Bloc countries agreed to respect human rights, including the rights embodied in the ICCPR and other human rights treaties they had signed. The Soviets resisted the human rights provisions during the negotiations, but finally yielded because they believed that the territorial guarantees were more important and that human rights could be managed. However, the human rights provisions turned out to be a major boost for dissident groups throughout the Eastern Bloc. Those groups set up Helsinki Committees, which monitored and criticized the human rights performance of their countries.

The Helsinki Accords may thus have given dissidents hope. Perhaps they believed that consent to the Helsinki Accords signaled a weakening of repression; perhaps it showed that some government officials believed that rights should be respected after all, and thus would give dissidents a sympathetic hearing, or at least not crack down as hard against political dissent as in the past. Or maybe dissidents believed that by entering into the Helsinki Accords, communist governments had boxed themselves in by signaling to their populations that they cared about rights, which may have made it more politically difficult for them to crack down on dissenters.

But it would be almost 20 years before the communist governments fell and were replaced by less repressive regimes. Nor did repression decline in a measurable sense in the years after Eastern Bloc countries entered into the Helsinki Accords. Eastern Bloc countries consistently received the worst Freedom House ratings, between 5 and 7, for more than a decade *after* the signing of the Helsinki Accords. Modest improvements began in some countries (Poland, Hungary) in the 1980s, while other countries (Bulgaria, Romania, Czechoslovakia) did not improve until later that decade. And it was not until 1990 that Freedom House ranked an Eastern Bloc county as "free," rather than "partly free" or "not free." Thus, if the human rights provisions of the Helsinki Accords changed the behavior of the Eastern Bloc governments, it could not have had a very large effect.

Histories of the Helsinki process make clear that whatever role domestic groups played in improving human rights in the communist countries, the major role was played by foreign countries, and, particularly, the United States. President Carter made human rights a focus of American policy, although he pursued it inconsistently; President Reagan linked human rights to his anti-communism, and used it as a cudgel for embarrassing the Soviet Union, while (like Carter) tolerating human rights violations by American allies. These efforts may have helped erode the image of the Soviet Union around the world, and weakened its influence among left-wing groups that had once been under its spell. More likely, however, the damage had been done by its own actions decades earlier—above all, by Stalin's excesses and their repudiation by Khrushchev.

Another popular view is that domestic litigation can cause countries to comply with human rights treaties. The constitutions of some countries provide that certain human rights treaties have constitutional status, potentially giving rise to litigation, though the extent to which such litigation is effective is poorly understood. In the United States, the government has forbidden courts to directly enforce human rights treaties against the government itself, but these treaties can occasionally have legal effect in indirect fashion. Sometimes, when a statute is ambiguous, a court may interpret the statute so as to avoid violating a treaty. But this happens rarely.

A more significant source of litigation is a law called the Alien Tort Statute, which gives courts jurisdiction over suits brought by aliens who were wrongfully injured by people or institutions in violation of international law, including international human rights law. As interpreted by the courts, the ATS does *not* give Americans the right to sue the U.S. (or any other) government for violating human rights treaties; nor does it give aliens the right to sue the U.S. (or any other) government for violating human rights treaties. Aliens can sue government officials (albeit subject to numerous conditions) for, say, torturing them; but as a practical matter, they cannot obtain damages unless those government officials own judicially attachable property in the United States, and they almost never do. The most successful lawsuits have targeted corporations that were complicit in the human rights violations of foreign governments—for example, an oil pipeline company that allegedly received protection from government troops which committed atrocities. But even these lawsuits usually fail because of the difficulty of showing complicity and disagreement as to whether a corporation can violate international law in the first place. Recently, the Supreme Court all but shut the door on such cases, based in part on a worry that ATS litigation offends foreign countries because it can influence how foreign companies behave in those countries, thus interfering with domestic regulation.[1]

5.3. AMBIGUITY AND INCONSISTENCY

There is another perspective on compliance, which is that the problem is not so much that states violate treaty terms but that the treaties do not create any meaningful obligations. This is so because the treaties are vague; they conflict with each other; and they conflict with other rules of international law. When legal rules are vague, one can easily argue that one complied with them even when one's conduct does not seem to advance the underlying purpose of the rules, which people will disagree about. When legal rules conflict, a person who is subject to them cannot be blamed for failing to comply with any one of them; at best, one can complain that the person did not act in good faith to resolve the conflict in the spirit of the laws, to "balance" the interests that are embodied in different human rights. Thus, a state that attempts to comply in good faith with the treaties would find itself thrown back on its own judgment as to how to advance the public good.

We already identified the vagueness problem in Chapter 2. For example, Article 19(2) of the ICCPR guarantees freedom of expression but then provides that states may curtail that right in the interest of morality and public order. None of these terms are defined. Many countries that have ratified the ICCPR prosecute people who criticize the government. While in the United States such prosecutions would violate the First Amendment, the governments in other countries argue that criticism of the government causes civil strife, disrespect for authority, or violation of moral values. European governments have jailed people who have engaged in hate speech against Muslims, Jews, and other minorities. Countless treaty terms are similarly vague.

The vagueness is compounded by internal inconsistencies in many human rights treaties. In addition to creating a right to work, the ICESCR creates rights to health care, education, and social welfare. States that seek to satisfy these rights must make tradeoffs. Because states have limited resources, money used to provide health care comes from education, or vice versa. The treaty provides no guidance as to how resources should be allocated among programs that advance different treaty rights.

Consider, for example, a country that has a budget of $10 billion. The government spends $5 billion on the military, $2 billion on health care, $2 billion on education, and $1 billion on welfare programs. Many citizens are poor, poorly educated, and in ill health. Does the country comply with the ICESCR? Should the government spend less money on the military—but doesn't that depend on whether it faces a legitimate foreign threat or needs the military for domestic order? Maybe the ICESCR requires the government to raise taxes and spend more money on health, education, and welfare. But how high should the taxes be raised?; what if higher taxes would reduce revenue because of tax evasion or negative effects on economic growth; or what if the public will not support higher taxes?

Should more money be spent on welfare and less on education and health care?

One could, in theory, solve the problem by stipulating that the rights to education and health care are "minimal" rights. But the treaties do not say this, it is not clear what "minimal" means, and if the rights were set at a level that any state could comply with, then the level would have to be so low as to be meaningless for the vast majority of states.

The Committee on Economic, Social and Cultural Rights initially recognized that some countries were too poor to satisfy all these rights, and ruled that those countries would nonetheless be in compliance with the ICESCR as long as they used best efforts to meet their obligations. Subsequently, the Committee ruled that all countries must supply a "minimum core" of those goods and services covered by the rights. But states ignored this interpretation. The South African Constitutional Court rejected the "minimum core obligation concept,"[2] pointing out that a treaty cannot require a state to do the impossible, and concluding that whether a country violates economic rights under the ICESCR depends "on such factors as the economic and social history of a country, its current circumstances, the prevalence of poverty, the availability of land, the degree of unemployment, and the fact of whether an individual lived in an urban or rural environment."[3] The Committee itself said:

> Thus, for example, a State party in which any significant number of individuals is deprived of essential foodstuffs, of essential primary health care, of basic shelter and housing, or of the most basic forms of education is, prima facie, failing to discharge its obligations under the Covenant.. . . By the same token, it must be noted that any assessment as to whether a State has discharged its minimum core obligation must also take account of resource constraints applying within the country concerned.[4]

The extent to which resources constraints modify the duty is not explained.

There are, to be sure, countries that incorporate economic rights into their constitutions. But courts rarely try to enforce those rights, noting that there is no principled way to do so. How to allocate resources among the various needs and demands is a political question, or at least not one that lends itself to judicial involvement. Courts instead treat social and economic constitutional rights as judicially unenforceable "aspirational" rights to be implemented by the government if it chooses. In a few countries, such as Brazil, courts have taken a more aggressive role, but with disappointing results. According to one scholar, the decision to provide judicial enforcement for the right to health in Brazil has resulted in thousands of cases by people claiming a right to high-cost medicines that the government has refused to supply on cost-effectiveness grounds, many of which are not even imported into the Brazilian market. Thus, recognition of a right to health led to cases brought by the relatively wealthy, not cases that have sought greater access to health care for the poor, no doubt because the poor do not have the resources to bring lawsuits.[5]

These problems with so-called positive or social rights are well known. Less well known is that the same problem exists for the "negative rights" in the ICCPR, such as the right not to be tortured. One might think that a state could comply with the prohibition on torture at no cost by refraining from torture. But it turns out that local police officials frequently engage in torture even though they are not authorized to do so. To stop torture, then, the government must not only enact laws, but must also invest resources in investigating allegations of torture, punishing torturers, and purging and retraining law enforcement. Thus, the key question for a state is how much of its resources it must devote to countering torture at the expense of building health clinics and public schools. The treaties provide no guidance as to how resources should be allocated. If there is no way to distinguish positive and negative rights, and we are skeptical about whether judges can enforce positive rights, then we ought to be skeptical about whether they can enforce negative rights as well. The real question is not the nature of the rights but the extent to which we can trust judges or other enforcing agents to distribute resources between competing rights.

There is yet another problem. Although not all treaty terms are vague, the actual legal effect of even specific norms is often ambiguous because they conflict with terms in other treaties as well as with broader norms of public international law. Consider sections 3 and 4 of Article 9 of the ICCPR:

> 3. Anyone arrested or detained on a criminal charge shall be brought promptly before a judge or other officer authorized by law to exercise judicial power and shall be entitled to trial within a reasonable time or to release. . . .
>
> 4. Anyone who is deprived of his liberty by arrest or detention shall be entitled to take proceedings before a court, in order that that court may decide without delay on the lawfulness of his detention and order his release if the detention is not lawful.

Whatever else these rights require, they do clearly prohibit a state from detaining people without charging them. Thus, many commentators accused the United States of violating the human rights of Al Qaeda and Taliban suspects by detaining them without charging them and taking them before a judge for a trial. However, the United States argued in response that the ICCPR does not apply to wartime conditions: the Geneva Conventions and other laws of war, which do not require the involvement of courts for detention, are *lex specialis*, and thus override human rights law.

The principle of lex specialis is well established in international (and domestic) law. Different sources of law conflict, and a principle is needed to resolve such conflicts. Many human rights advocates believe that the human rights treaties provide a moral minimum that other bodies of law can never supersede, much like the rights in the U.S. Bill of Rights. However, the human rights treaties themselves do not say this, nor does any other authoritative source of international law. There is no clear resolution of the dispute between the United States and its critics.

Another major challenge to conventional understandings of human rights comes from the "right to development," which has been strongly advocated by China and has been embodied in various legal instruments though not a formal treaty. According to China, the right to development is essentially a right *not* to comply with human rights norms that interfere with the ability of poor countries to grow economically and eliminate poverty. Thus, it is open to China to argue that if it granted the political rights in the ICCPR to its citizens, then political turmoil would result, including possibly civil war, with the result that economic growth would stop and poverty would advance. The argument is not a crazy one. China's authoritarian government has eliminated poverty for hundreds of millions of people over the last 30 years. In light of the lack of democratic traditions in China, and the extraordinary political turmoil that existed in China until fairly recently, there is a risk that if China were to comply with the ICCPR, civil war rather than democracy would result. Of course, this has always been the argument of authoritarians. The point is that the argument is not foreclosed by international law, and even democratic or semi-democratic governments have embraced the right to development.

The right to development puts in stark relief another problem for human rights, which is the proliferation or *hypertrophy of human rights*. The original idea of human rights is that they would protect only the most significant human interests—in being alive, being free of pain, being free to speak, and so on. But the number of internationally recognized rights has increased exponentially. Some of them—the right to "periodic holidays with pay," say—have been met with skepticism even by people who support the human rights project. The mockery may reflect a certain nervousness. It can't be the case that all human interests are protected by international law, but where to draw the line? Some scholars have tried to respond by creating a hierarchy of rights, arguing that while all the human rights are rights, some are more important, like the right not to be tortured. But this view has been attacked and has had no practical consequences.

A review of the major international human rights treaties reveals that treaties purport to guarantee more than 300 separate human rights, ranging from the right to inherit, to the right to have an interpreter in official proceedings, to the right to freedom of movement, to the right to leisure, to the right to privacy, to the right to join trade unions. The list, which can be found in the Appendix, goes on and on. The number of human rights increased from 20 in 1975, to 100 in 1980, to 175 in 1990, to 300 today.

The hypertrophy of human rights highlights the problem of tradeoffs. If there were only a few rights—for example, the right not to be tortured and the right not to be arbitrarily detained—it would seem simple enough to determine whether states comply with them. But when there are hundreds of rights, states must make complex tradeoffs. States have limited resources—understood broadly to include funds, political will, and institutional capacity—and must allocate them to different projects. A project to reduce torture like a training program for local police necessarily uses funds that could be used to protect religious freedom or increase schooling. The dilemma for human rights enforcers is that they cannot demand that states comply with all rights perfectly, but if they do not, then they have no basis for criticizing a country's decision to allocate more resources to satisfy one rather than another.

The hypertrophy of human rights results from fundamental disagreement about the public good. The problem is that if significant resources are already devoted to reducing torture, and the marginal dollar has little effect because torture is entrenched in society, then the marginal dollar may be more wisely spent on reducing pollution or strengthening the military or improving the quality of the roads. To justify these allocations of the marginal dollar in the language of human rights, governments must insist the people have a human right not only to be free of torture, but to be free of pollution, foreign threats, or low-quality roads (or more broadly, poor infrastructure that blocks economic development). This is why human rights keep proliferating and in this way render each other meaningless for constraining behavior. The human rights treaties provide no guidance for allocating that dollar, and so instead governments must fall back on making tradeoffs based on their conception of the public good. Human rights treaties can be no more than vague encouragement for governments to govern well—but it is hard to believe that governments already inclined to govern well or governments not so inclined, would change their behavior as a consequence of such encouragement. Because the treaties send conflicting signals and do not explain how one is to make tradeoffs, they could not provide guidance even to a government that was motivated to take them seriously.

This problem is related to a much discussed issue in the literature as to whether human rights should be limited so as to protect a narrow set of human interests (like the interest in not being tortured) or should include a much larger set of interests. Michael Ignatieff, for example, argues that human rights should be understood to consist of a limited set of negative rights sufficient to protect people from "violence and abuse."[6] He has been taken to task by critics who have pointed out the absence of any normative basis for limiting rights in this way, which simply endorses one controversial strand of the Western tradition of rights. Whoever is right (and I believe the critics are right), the existing human rights regime is vastly more comprehensive. It is not limited to prohibiting the worst violations of negative rights, or to negative rights at all; its inclusion of positive rights of all kinds ensures that countries can justify violations of negative rights as necessary tradeoffs for reducing poverty and securing other goods for their populations. Protecting people from "violence and abuse" means protecting them from starvation, insecurity, and illiteracy, all of which are springboards for private violence directed against innocent people. Securing the negative liberties is neither a necessary nor sufficient condition for achieving those ends. Human rights cannot be limited to negative rights because negative rights are not the most important, or the only ones that count.

The hypertrophy of human rights—the proliferation of human rights treaties, of interpretations of those treaties that find new human rights, of claims about the existence of still more human rights in customary international law—does *not* represent a triumph of human rights, and the erosion of sovereignty, as is so often claimed. It represents more nearly the opposite. The more human rights there are, and thus the greater the variety of human interests that are protected, the more that the human rights system collapses into an undifferentiated welfarism in which all interests must be taken seriously for the sake of the public good.

Ambiguity matters because countries that are not bound by specific legal rules can do nearly anything they want without violating the law. Countries and groups that try to enforce human rights law must select among the rights and enforce the ones that they care the most about. The U.S. State Department, for example, focuses on the major ICCPR rights, and ignores most economic, social, and cultural rights. Similarly, NGOs focus on whatever rights they care about.

Human Rights Watch disregards economic, social, and cultural rights not because they are intrinsically unimportant, but because HRW can provoke a greater public reaction when it identifies specific abusers and victims. According to Kenneth Roth, the executive director of HRW, it is hard to blame anyone in particular for poverty, but it is possible to blame government officials for torture and disappearances. Roth is making a practical argument about public psychology, based on his experience with when HRW reports strike a chord with the public and when they do not—a point that is really about what works politically and what does not work politically, as opposed to what the law requires. To the extent HRW successfully pressures governments, this just means that those governments may transfer resources from poverty prevention to torture prevention. Whether or not this is a good use of resources seems to be a matter of institutional indifference to HRW.

5.4. WHY INTERNATIONAL ORGANIZATIONS ARE NO SOLUTION

Domestic legal systems contain numerous ambiguous and conflicting laws, and yet these laws are often effective in changing behavior. The major reason that ambiguous laws exist in the first place is that the legislature finds it difficult to anticipate future events that it seeks to regulate. Rather than provide detailed rules that govern every possible future contingency, it provides vague guidelines to regulatory agencies or courts, and expects them to issue more precise rules as events unfold, and to reconcile legislative enactments that are in tension with each other.

An example from American law is the Sherman Antitrust Act, a short statute that prohibits people from engaging in "restraint of trade" and from "monopoliz[ing]." Congress left these crucial terms undefined; over decades, courts and regulatory agencies have created thousands of rules that fill in their meaning. These rules distinguish, for example, ordinary contracts, which by their nature restrain trade, and contracts among competitors to fix prices. Although most statutes are more detailed than the Sherman Act, in the modern regulatory state huge swaths of lawmaking are left to regulatory agencies and courts.

It should be clear that, in principle, international courts or regulatory agencies could play a similar role in giving content to the human rights that are incorporated in human rights treaties and resolving conflicts between them. Indeed, one of the main purposes of setting up the various international human rights organizations—the treaty committees, the UN Commission and Council, the OHCHR—was to provide a mechanism for specifying the content of international human rights. But international human rights laws are as vague today as they were when they were drafted. None of these institutions has managed to issue authoritative interpretations, as domestic courts have for domestic law. Why not?

To answer this question, let's begin with the ECHR, which is the world's most successful international human rights institution. In Chapter 2, I discussed Hirst v. United Kingdom, the case in which the ECHR held that depriving prisoners of the right to vote may violate their rights under the European Convention of Human Rights. The European Convention nowhere says that prisoners have the right to vote; it instead refers generally to the right to the franchise and to political participation. The ECHR's holding must have thus been a surprise to the UK; the holding certainly could not have been anticipated when the UK ratified the European Convention.

This type of expansive interpretation is not uncommon among domestic constitutional courts. The U.S. Supreme Court's interpretations of the First Amendment as well as other vague provisions in the Constitution—rights to "due process," for example—similarly have involved rulings that could not have been anticipated by the drafters but that reflect evolving norms as well as the ideological propensities of the justices. But the difference between the Supreme Court and the ECHR is that the Supreme Court is an American institution, staffed by American justices, who are appointed by American politicians. From the perspective of the UK or any of its other members, the ECHR is a foreign institution, staffed mostly by foreigners, who are appointed mostly by foreign politicians. While Americans feel that they can trust the Supreme Court to rule in the public interest, it is harder for the British to know whether the ECHR will rule in the UK's interest. The Supreme Court justices understand American cultural and political norms and live in the country to which their rulings apply. For the non-British members of the ECHR, the UK is a foreign country where people do things differently. Thus, American Supreme Court justices have more legitimacy for Americans than the ECHR judges have for the British.

This is not to say that the ECHR cannot succeed. But it is crucial to understand that the ECHR has done as well as it has because it operates in a regional setting in which there is a moral and political convergence among most member states. The ECHR developed a doctrine known as the "margin of appreciation," according to which it provides some but not complete deference to laws of the member states. For example, in the Handyside case, the ECHR turned away a challenge to a prosecution under the UK Obscene Publications Act of a publisher who tried to publish a sex education book for children. In explaining why the prosecution did not violate the freedom of expression article of the European Convention, the Court noted:

> By reason of their direct and continuous contact with the vital forces of their countries, State authorities are in principle in a better position than the international judge to give an opinion

on the exact content of these requirements as well as the "necessity" of a "restriction" or "penalty" intended to meet them.[7]

The Court concluded that the relevant government enjoys a margin of appreciation, albeit not an unlimited one. One reason it gave for finding the margin of appreciation was that the domestic laws of the member states were not consistent, and hence that those states lacked "a uniform European conception of morals." Over the years, it has become clear that the margin of appreciation narrows when most states agree that some activity violates human rights, so that the Court's function is to mop up outliers, much as the U.S. Supreme Court does in its Eighth Amendment jurisprudence, where the "unusual" in "cruel and unusual" is defined by reference to the practice of most (U.S.) states.

The margin of appreciation is thus a device for intervening when member states largely agree on an outcome, and for refraining from intervention otherwise. Accordingly, it enables the Court to track majority or, indeed, supermajority, views, and thus retain its political support. The court can actively rule against outliers because most Europeans share a moral outlook.

The margin of appreciation has been rejected by international tribunals despite calls for its application internationally, where the need to respect national differences is significantly more pressing than in Europe. There is a good reason why international tribunals reject the margin of appreciation: if they applied it the way the ECHR did, it would deprive those tribunals of the power to condemn more than a handful of countries, those that could be identified as true outliers in a world of extreme heterogeneity.

Consider, for example, the ECHR's jurisprudence on the rights of gays and lesbians. The ECHR ruled that the margin of appreciation does not justify Russia's refusal to permit a gay pride march in Moscow, but does allow member states to refuse to recognize same-sex marriage. The different outcomes reflect different levels of consensus. Most member states recognize the right to assembly, but they disagree about same-sex marriage. With 47 member states, including Poland, Russia, and Turkey, no consensus will be reached anytime soon. And yet if the entire world belonged to the ECHR, it would be hard to say that the right to freedom of assembly would encompass gay pride marches, as no such marches are permitted in many countries.

When one moves from the regional ECHR to truly international human rights institutions, like the human rights committees and the Human Rights Council, the distance between the national and cultural character of the body and the national and cultural character of the citizens of a particular member state becomes even more vast. A human rights committee, for example, is staffed with representatives from not just the European countries, but also from Africa, South America, Asia, and North America. This body is much more foreign from the standpoint of, say, the British, than the ECHR is. After all, the ECHR is dominated by people from places like Germany, France, and the Netherlands—where Western-style human rights are entrenched. The human rights committee is a far more diverse place, which means that the average member will have more difficulty understanding or sympathizing with the UK perspective, and will for that reason also be regarded with even more suspicion by the British than the ECHR is. That is why the committees are starved of resources and frequently ignored.

The defamation of religion controversy illustrates these themes. In 1999 the Organization of the Islamic Conference, a group of (currently) 56 Muslim countries, introduced a resolution at a meeting of the Human Rights Commission that was entitled "Defamation of Islam" and called on the UN to monitor "attacks against Islam and attempts to defame it." The OIC believed that the resolution was necessary to counter what it saw as anti-Islamic sentiment in the West. Western diplomats were able to change the name of the resolution to "Defamation of Religion," but because figures in other major religions have not argued that criticism of those religions should be banned, defamation of religion continued to be associated with Islam. The Commission approved the resolution, and additional resolutions were approved in subsequent years, including after the 9/11 attack, and after a Danish newspaper published cartoons of Mohammed in 2005. In that year, the UN General Assembly also passed a resolution condemning defamation of religion.

Below I list the countries that voted in favor of or against, or abstained with respect to, two resolutions before the UN Commission (in 2001) and the UN Council (in 2010). The 2001 resolution was passed by a vote of 25 to 18, with 9 abstentions. The 2010 resolution was passed by a vote of 20 to 17, with 8 abstentions.

2001 Resolution

In favor: Algeria, Argentina, Brazil, Cameroon, China, Colombia, Costa Rica, Cuba, Ecuador, Indonesia, Kenya, Libyan Arab Jamahiriya, Madagascar, Malaysia, Mauritius, Mexico, Niger, Pakistan, Peru, Qatar, Russia, Saudi Arabia, Senegal, Syrian Arab Republic, Thailand, Uruguay, Venezuela, Vietnam.

Against: Belgium, Canada, Czech Republic, France, Germany, Italy, Japan, Latvia, Norway, Poland, Portugal, Romania, Spain, United Kingdom, United States of America.

Abstaining: Burundi, Guatemala, India, Liberia, Nigeria, Republic of Korea, South Africa, Swaziland, Zambia.

2010 Resolution

In favor: Bahrain, Bangladesh, Bolivia, Burkina Faso, China, Cuba, Djibouti, Egypt, Indonesia, Jordan, Kyrgyzstan, Nicaragua, Nigeria, Pakistan, Philippines, Qatar, Russia, Saudi Arabia, Senegal, South Africa

Against: Argentina, Belgium, Chile, France, Hungary, Italy, Mexico, Netherlands, Norway, South Korea, Slovakia, Slovenia, Ukraine, United Kingdom, United States of America, Uruguay, Zambia.

Abstaining: Bosnia and Herzegovina, Brazil, Cameroon, Ghana, India, Japan, Madagascar, Mauritius.

A glance confirms that predominantly Western democracies voted against the defamation of religion resolutions, while the rest of the world tended to support the resolutions.

The OIC and its supporters argued that criticism of Islam (and other religions) violated several provisions of the human rights treaties. Article 18 of the Universal Declaration provides that "everyone has the right to freedom of thought, conscience and religion." Article 19 of the ICCPR provides that freedom of expression may "be subject to certain restrictions [including] for the respect of the rights or reputations of others." Article 20 of the same treaty provides that "any advocacy of national, racial or religious hatred that constitutes incitement to discrimination, hostility or violence shall be prohibited by law." The OIC argued that anti-Islamic advocacy, including disregard of the Muslim taboo against depictions of the prophet, amounts to interference with the practice of the faith and incitement to discrimination.

Critics of defamation of religion argue that treaty provisions give pride of place to freedom of expression and permit censorship under only the narrowest of conditions, but the fact is that many Western countries other than the United States practice censorship—for example, of Nazi-related advocacy and various types of hostile speech directed at religious and sexual minorities. To the extent that the UN human rights bodies are delegated the power to interpret and develop human rights norms, it would seem that by now Western countries would be bound by the defamation of religion theory.

Except that they are not. Western countries reject defamation of religion, and thus they reject the authority of the human rights bodies to impose this norm on them. And taking the Western perspective (which most readers of this book will share), it is easy to understand why the United States, Netherlands, and France would refuse to delegate legal authority to an international body that operates by majority rule. Why should we in the West accept norms governing speech based on theological and political imperatives that we do not agree with? And so it should also be easy to understand why Saudi Arabia, China, and Indonesia would not want to delegate legal authority to an international body where they, too, could be outvoted on issues that matter to them. Just as Westerners refuse to bow to non-Western norms they disagree with, non-Westerners refuse to bow to Western norms they disagree with. And why shouldn't they? Why should countries that recognize norms that most or nearly all countries refuse to recognize be forced to abandon their own norms and recognize those that more widely prevail? The margin of appreciation, if applied consistently, would block the emergence of new, more liberal norms that shock the orthodoxy, as well as non-liberal norms that seem retrogressive.

Another example is also instructive. In the 1990s various international bodies (including the British Privy Council and the Human Rights Committee) held that certain procedures relating to capital punishment in several Caribbean nations violated the ICCPR. The decisions were unpopular, and the governments responded by withdrawing from treaties and other instruments that subjected them to the jurisdiction of international courts.[8] They did not withdraw from the ICCPR itself, which illustrates that governments can live with treaties that contain norms they can explain away or ignore. They cannot live with judicial bodies that issue orders that they do not want to obey, and so they keep international bodies weak, do not set them up, or, as in this example, withdraw from them. The events in the Caribbean also illustrate the weakness of the ICCPR, and by extension all human rights treaties, in constraining states when they are not implemented by independent judicial bodies. Governments appear to incur political costs from defying the orders of international judicial bodies whose jurisdiction they agree to, but not (or less so) from defying their treaty obligations when there is no judicial body to interpret and apply them.

An international human rights body is an agent of the nations that establish it. The nations want their agent to serve certain purposes. Ideally, the agent would encourage or even compel the parties of the treaty to comply with the treaty and end their human rights violations. The nations thus should instruct the agent to monitor the states, and use whatever means seem appropriate to bring them in line. But this has not happened with the human rights bodies. The human rights treaties papered over significant differences by using vague language and by piling on rights. When it comes time for implementation, the human rights agencies are put in the position of giving content to those provisions. Only then does it become clear that the level of agreement is shallow. Agencies must then take a position and risk disagreement and repudiation from states whose views they reject.

Countries must have understood these problems from the beginning—for only that explains why they gave the human rights bodies so little power compared to the power they give to their domestic courts. In particular, the human rights violating states have worked again and again to ensure that the human rights bodies cannot condemn specific countries for specific practices, or at least can do so only in limited circumstances, and in such a way as to have no legal or political effect. And when they find themselves subject to legally binding orders from international courts, they can always withdraw from jurisdiction, as the Caribbean countries did.

Thus, while countries recognized from the beginning of the modern era of human rights that international organizations were necessary for implementing human rights treaties—for giving vague terms content, resolving conflicts, monitoring countries, and pressuring them to comply with the treaties—countries also realized that agencies that possessed enough power to serve these functions would pose a threat to their interests. The compromise has been a system of agencies that are given no formal legal powers, and are too weak, underfunded, and dependent on avoiding offense to provide an effective system of enforcement. Indeed, while the inadequate resources of the committees are well known, the response of states has been not to strengthen the institutional system but to keep adding human rights treaties with new substantive obligations, which further overwhelm the infrastructure.

5.5. A FAILURE OF WILL

I have argued that the reason human rights law has failed to improve respect for human rights is that the law is weak—the treaties are vague and inconsistent, and the institutions are balkanized, starved of resources, and unequipped with legal authority. Why have states failed to create stronger law and more robust institutions? Below I consider two possible answers.

People don't care (much) about the human rights of foreigners. Many states have authoritarian governments or traditions that lack human rights norms; in these states, governments are under little pressure domestically to improve their enforcement of human rights. These states have no incentive to exert pressure on foreign countries to improve their human rights, and rarely do. Consider, for example, China, Russia, and Saudi Arabia. China and Russia do not take much interest in the well-being of foreigners. Saudi Arabia does, but by financing madrassas in foreign countries that teach fundamentalist Islamic doctrine, not human rights. Many other states—much of the vast developing world—have more democratic governments and more open societies, and respect some human rights internally. But their populations are focused inward, on the difficult process of state-building and development, and so do not exert much pressure on their governments to improve human rights elsewhere in the world.

That leaves the West—the United States, the European countries, Canada, Australia, and a few others. The populations of these countries are wealthy and mostly liberal. Their governments provide foreign aid, and many private citizens devote time and money to help foreigners in foreign countries. But these efforts are minimal. One study suggests that if the amount of foreign aid represents how much Americans care about foreigners, then Americans think of a foreign life in a poor country as 1/2,000 as valuable as an American life.[9] This doesn't mean that people lack altruism; it means that their altruism is mostly confined to co-nationals.

Thus, populations in democracies put little pressure on their governments to give aid to foreigners, either in the form of development projects or human rights enforcement, and governments in democracies must respect the wishes of voters. Indeed, most Western efforts to provide aid and promote human rights are driven by instrumental concerns about global stability, or efforts to advance geopolitical interests. But supporting human rights does not always achieve these goals. They are better achieved by cooperating with authoritarian countries like China, Russia, and Saudi Arabia.

The EU has been effective at encouraging countries at the European periphery to improve human rights by dangling the carrot of EU membership, but it is not potent enough to exert pressure on Russia, China, and other countries that are powerful or far away from the European continent. The current resurgence of authoritarianism in Hungary provides an important test case of the ability of the European liberal democracies to compel foreign countries to abide by human rights norms. If Europeans cannot even compel a small, financially dependent country in their midst to comply with human rights, then one must infer that they do not care enough about human rights to devote substantial resources to them. The point is not that Western states discount human rights; it is that they balance their interest in promoting human rights with their interest in political stability and economic growth, and casual as well as rigorous empiricism suggests that the interest in promoting human rights receives minimal weight in the balance. Trade provides a useful counterpoint. States care enough about their economic interests that they put a great deal of pressure on other countries to abide by trade treaties.

Thus, while states are willing to enter into human rights treaties and hope that they will exert positive pressure on human rights violators, they are not willing to put significant resources into enforcing those treaties. More to the point, they tolerate the treaty regime because the ambiguities and conflicts in and among the treaties provide countries with plenty of freedom of action—permitting Western countries both to restrict human rights domestically when necessary, and to refrain, without appearing to repudiate their treaty obligations, from putting too much pressure on foreign rights violators. The key move was to enter into these treaties without providing for strong international organizations to enforce them, so that—unlike in domestic law—countries can work around the treaties without defying specific legal orders.

Enforcement is too hard. Coercing a foreign state is not easy. Consider an enforcing state that seeks to cause a target state to stop torturing people. The enforcing state could threaten to cut off trade, terminate diplomatic relations, refuse to grant visas to visitors from the target state, freeze the funds of the target state, issue arrest warrants for the leaders of the target state, launch a military invasion, and so on. All of these activities are highly costly. If the enforcing state cuts off trade, then it no longer benefits from trade, and if the target increases trade with other countries, it is the enforcer rather than the target that ends up isolated. If it cuts off diplomatic relations, then it will become harder to cooperate with the state on issues of mutual interest. The target state may have no funds in the enforcing state; and if it does, then the enforcing state that freezes funds too often may cause other states to withdraw funds, making it harder to do business.

Worse for the enforcing state, its enforcement efforts may drive the target state into the arms of rivals and enemies, who provide the diplomatic support and cooperative benefits that the enforcing state tries to deprive it of. Indeed, even friendly countries may free ride on the enforcing states' efforts, maintaining their own cooperative relationships with the target state while the enforcing state bears all the burdens. The prospect of free riding will discourage any state from taking the role of enforcer in the first place. And as we saw earlier, efforts to overcome collective action problems through the construction of international institutions have foundered because the collective action problem reemerges within the operation of those institutions.

The people-don't-care and enforcement-is-too-hard problems are connected. If people cared more, then they would bear the costs of enforcement; and if enforcement were cheap and easy, then people would bear the cost of enforcement even if they cared only a little. But they don't care much and enforcement is hard, which is why serious efforts to enforce human rights are extremely rare, and take place only in response to the worst atrocities such as genocide, and, as we saw in Rwanda, not always then.

Still, these two explanations are not entirely satisfactory. For one thing, they assume that people do not care very much about foreigners, but then another question arises—why not? People are willing to make sacrifices for co-nationals even though they never meet them; why shouldn't this altruism extend beyond borders? The same two explanations could be used to show why domestic constitutional enforcement is not possible; but in fact, it is possible. We must continue to look for explanations.

5.6. THE PROBLEM OF EPISTEMIC UNCERTAINTY

I now turn to a deeper problem with international human rights law—the problem of epistemic uncertainty—which I will try to explain by drawing on a domestic analogy: the problems with judicial enforcement of constitutional rights. This might seem to be an odd approach. Judicial enforcement of constitutional rights, represented most fully by the U.S. system, is for some people the inspiration for international human rights law. However, I am going to argue the other way around: that when one thinks carefully about judicial enforcement of constitutional rights, it becomes easier to see what is wrong with international human rights law.

A simplified picture of U.S. constitutional law begins with the idea that Americans enjoy certain "rights." These rights are recognized by the Constitution, either directly in the text, or indirectly in judicial interpretations, or both. The rights protect important human interests. When the government makes policy, it must take those interests into account. It may be that in some cases, the rights are "absolute," in the sense that the government may never disregard those interests. For example, perhaps the government is never permitted to impose a cruel and unusual punishment on someone. In most cases, however, we think that rights are not "absolute." The interest in freedom of expression is very strong, so the government may limit that freedom only for good reasons (for example, to protect someone from fraud or defamation). Courts do not normally say that the government may violate the right if there are strong interests on the other side; instead, the right is defined as protected unless overridden by compelling factors on the other side.

A crucial feature of U.S. constitutional law is that the judiciary is charged with the task of ensuring that the government respect the rights in the Constitution. The idea that (unelected) judges may strike down laws that violate the Constitution sits uneasily with democratic commitments, and theorists have labored to reconcile these two ideals. One view is that democracy works only as long as certain rules are respected, and the judge's task is to enforce those rules. For example, judges should prevent elected officials from entrenching their authority by abolishing elections, restricting who can vote, or prohibiting criticism of their actions. Another view is that democracy sometimes works too well, and the majority oppresses the minority. The task of the judges is to protect the rights of the minority to enjoy freedom, property, and other basic human goods even if they are repeatedly outvoted on issues of public policy. A third view is that constitutional norms reflect strong political commitments that should prevail over normal politics, because people take constitutional deliberation and constitution-making more seriously than ordinary politics.

It is easy to see how this thinking could influence the international human rights movement. In some ways, the argument for international human rights is even more compelling than the argument for domestically enforced constitutional rights. The reason is that the international human rights regime applies to non-democratic states as well as democratic states and it may seem more compelling to insist that a dictator not violate people's rights than to say that a democracy may not violate people's rights. But in other ways, the analogy breaks down. In the United States, courts are regarded (rightly or wrongly) as neutral arbiters, and so can be trusted to enforce rights fairly (on this, I will say more below). The international human rights regime depends mainly on enforcement by states, which are the same entities subject to the rights regime and for that reason may not be trusted with a task that requires neutrality and fairness.

Rather than press this point, however, I want to suggest why it is that even if the constitutional analogy is taken seriously, it provides weak support for the human rights system, and indeed does the opposite—points out flaws in the premises of the human rights system.

The first problem with constitutional adjudication is epistemic. Policy is complicated, and judicial review requires courts to evaluate the policy rationales for statutes. To take a recent case, in District of Columbia v. Heller,[10] the Supreme Court was required to decide whether a gun control law violated the Second Amendment right to bear arms. The Court faced two closely connected questions: how to define the right (for example, does it extend to machine guns?) and how to evaluate statutes that appear in tension with the right (for example, does a registration statute put too much of a burden on the gun owner?). To answer these questions, the Court must make a judgment about how dangerous certain weapons are, and how burdensome the various legal obligations are. These are not questions one can answer by interpreting legal materials. They are empirical questions that must be answered (ideally) by analyzing data, or (more usually) by consulting anecdotes, common experience, intuition, and the like.

Are courts in a good position to answer these questions? They can certainly demand that litigants provide the best evidence available. But ultimately judges are in no better position to evaluate the data than legislators are, and probably worse—as legislators equip themselves with expert staffs who specialize in different policy domains. An even greater problem is that most judges lack any political sense.

Federal judges are appointed and serve for life, and so are not subject to electoral pressure. Most have little or no political experience. This ensures that they are not buffeted by the political winds, but also that they lack a strong sense of what people really care about. Constitutional doctrine typically turns on, among other things, the strength of a government's interest in some outcome, and the government's interest is generally derived from the public interest. If people care deeply about crime, then gun control laws may well serve their interests even if they have only marginal effects on the level of crime. If people care deeply about self-defense and hunting, then gun control laws that have marginal effects on crime will not serve their interests. The license to carry a concealed weapon might seem justified in one place where traditions ensure that people use guns responsibly, but not in another place where too many guns already flood the streets. Judges are in a weak position to make these determinations.

Indeed, it is rarely appreciated in legal scholarship just how serious this problem is. Judges must contend with the fact that people's political interests and preferences are private information, which they have no incentive to disclose truthfully in court, where advocates exaggerate in order to advance their clients' claims. Faced with noise from both directions, judges have little choice but to fall back on their own experience, supplemented with whatever data might exist. By contrast, elections compel people to reveal some private information by punishing them with an adverse outcome if they fail to do so. Politicians seek reelection and so have a strong incentive to learn from their constituents what they care about and how much, and to embody those views into policy. And while many factors—including financial donations to campaigns—may distort their incentives, politicians' fates are still tied more closely to the interests of the people than are those of judges.

This argument carries over to human rights. Even if governments tried to comply in good faith with human rights treaties, it does not follow that human rights outcomes would improve. Governance is a highly complex activity that is vulnerable to the law of unintended consequences. A government that stops using harsh methods of repression may be unable to stop an insurgency, which develops into a civil war, during which people suffer significantly more than they did when the government used harsh methods of repression. Many people will suffer at the hands of insurgents, and although the harm inflicted on them will not be classified as a violation of the human rights treaties because the government did not inflict the harm, the net outcome for people is just as bad, or worse. Some civil wars last decades and kill millions.

But even when such extreme outcomes do not result, efforts to comply with human rights norms can have perverse effects. Governments that abolish the death penalty may end up spurring the police to engage in extrajudicial killings so that they can keep order. A government that woodenly attempts to comply with the right to work may end up causing inflation or other disruptions to the economy that produce long-term harms worse than the joblessness that provoked the intervention.

Governments do not need human rights treaties to tell them to build medical clinics and schools. One might argue that they do not build enough clinics and schools, or insufficiently good clinics or schools, but how is one to know? Perhaps mortality is high and literacy is low, but high or low compared to what? Many countries are too poor to build many clinics and schools, and other countries have other legitimate priorities. To finance more buildings, one needs more money, which means raising taxes, taking on debt, or cutting spending in some other area. The public may be unwilling to pay higher taxes, or it may be impossible to collect more taxes given the existing enforcement system. It may be difficult or impossible or unwise to take on more debt. Even if the government collects more money, it may be more wisely spent on police, military protection, environmental cleanups, development projects, and so on.

The analogy to judicial review of domestic constitutions is even weaker because no international institution plays the role of the domestic courts. States enforce human rights treaties against states, which means that one state or a small group of states (typically, the United States and some European states) must decide how to interpret human rights treaties in the course of condemning (or not) the practices of another state. Take the issue of female genital cutting. It may be possible to apply human rights provisions "neutrally" to this practice, but it is difficult for Western countries to evaluate this practice in a dispassionate way because it violates deeply rooted Western norms. It would be even harder for these countries to predict how a prohibition on this practice would play out over time—whether it would, for example, lead to political turmoil that causes more harm than good. Finally, unlike courts, enforcing states will take into account domestic and international political pressures, and so will likely enforce the norms in a way that responds to those pressures rather than in a way that respects the law. It is, after all, distrust of the motives of governments that provides the basis for judicial review in the first place. And so if we distrust governments in the context of domestic constitutional litigation, we should distrust governments of enforcing states that claim to be enforcing human rights treaties as much as the governments of target states that are said to violate them.

If all this is true, then how is it possible for domestic courts to function effectively? After all, as I noted earlier, domestic courts are called on to make policy tradeoffs of a highly complex nature. If (domestic) constitutional law can work in this way, why can't international human rights law as well?

There are several reasons. First, courts (at least in Western countries) are reasonably independent institutions, and there are strong norms and expectations that judges decide cases neutrally. Even if they make errors, the errors will not systematically favor one political faction over another. By contrast, human rights are enforced by states (or international organizations controlled by states), and they have strong incentives to interpret human rights so as to advance their own interests, rather than in such a way that takes account of the complexity of policy tradeoffs in specific countries.

Second, American courts are staffed by Americans, who live in the United States and have a reasonably good understanding of American norms and institutions, even if they may lack a politician's sensitivity to public opinion. When they interpret the Constitution, they do so with an eye toward what is reasonable under prevailing conditions. But when states and international organizations try to enforce human rights in a particular state, the enforcers are usually foreigners, who have little experience with the target state. Foreign practices may seem hideous or inexplicable because the enforcers lack familiarity with them.

Third, most Western countries incorporate political checks on judges. In this respect, the United States is an outlier, as it is difficult to correct constitutional interpretations issued by the Supreme Court. Most countries allow their governments to override constitutional interpretations that seriously offend the public. But even in the United States (as well as in other countries), political officials can influence the course of constitutional law by appointing judges with the "appropriate" ideology, choosing which cases to bring and which to defend, and controlling the jurisdiction of the courts. There is always a back-and-forth between the political system and the judicial system, which allows the political system to correct some of the judiciary's errors. And all of this takes place within the context of democracy, where popular sovereignty is taken for granted.

But human rights laws lack this sophisticated institutional organization. The major states that enforce human rights laws cannot be forced to abandon or modify their interpretations, and they rarely do. It is true that target states can resist interpretations they dislike, but this reflects the weakness of human rights law, not its capacity for self-correction. If states can simply ignore interpretations they dislike, how could the treaties influence them? Most people in the world pay little attention to international human rights law, and do not try to make their voices heard about it. The world lacks authoritative institutions through which people or governments can impose a political check on the powerful states that enforce human rights law.

In sum, human rights law can be seen as a way to settle significant controversies about the human good, based on the notion that human beings possess enough knowledge about the undesirability of certain types of government behavior that they can rule them out. But conceptions of the human good change, and ideas about how best to trade off human values and how to implement them through government policy are constantly evolving as people gain information, test and discard proposals, observe experiments in other places, and so on. Because of the peculiar requirements of international cooperation, the international human rights institutions lack authoritative agencies that can modify rights in response to changing mores and the growth of empirical knowledge. The result is a system that is both rigid and vague, unresponsive to the needs of governments and populations, and thus ultimately plagued by circumvention on the part of the states it is supposed to bind.

5.7. THE IMPORTANCE OF POLITICAL PARTICIPATION

In much of the U.S. literature on constitutional law, the accepted view is that courts interpret rights that are embodied in the

Constitution and then enforce them by striking down legislation that conflicts with them. Thus, the process of recognizing rights involves the ordinary tools of legal interpretation, and the rights possess legal authority because they were ratified by the founding generation and the subsequent generations that ratified constitutional amendments. Some scholars believe that constitutional rights are only those that can be found in the original text and the amendments, while others believe that rights have been added to the Constitution through a process of judicial and political development, but both sides agree that constitutional democracy requires judicial review of laws and executive actions to ensure that they do not violate individual rights or any of the "structural" elements of the Constitution.

This is a highly simplified view of constitutional interpretation.[11] Because of the ambiguity of the rights in constitutional documents, courts must necessarily act as more than passive interpreters, and in practice have expanded and invented rights in response to the needs of their times. For example, until the New Deal the Supreme Court recognized rights to private property that put limits on federal and state regulation of working conditions and wages. In response in part to political pressure, the Court later abandoned this view so that legislation that was considered socially desirable could be put into effect. Since the 1950s and 1960s, the Court has created numerous rights for religious, racial, and ethnic minorities; political dissenters; criminal defendants; women; and gun owners—rights that had not previously been recognized.

But there is often just as much political dispute about the foundational rights that limit governmental activity as there is about ordinary policy. In the United States, large coalitions disagree profoundly and in good faith about whether there is or is not a constitutional right to undergo an abortion, to possess guns, and to marry a same-sex partner. And there is even more disagreement along the margins—for example, if there is a constitutional right to possess guns, is that right violated by a ban on machine guns or a law that requires registration of handguns?

Sometimes, the constitutional text anchors these debates, sometimes it does not. Many constitutional rights—for example, the rights to travel and to marry—are nowhere mentioned in the text of the Constitution. It is clear that the text does not determine the rights that are recognized by courts. Supreme Court justices recognize new rights and discard old rights based on legally constrained but ultimately moral-political determinations stemming from their own ideologies. Presidents nominate ideologically compatible lawyers to the Court for just this reason. Once one recognizes that rights emerge from democratic deliberation, and that the public asks Congress to embody them in legislation, then judicial review of that legislation begins to seem like usurpation of the public's right to political participation.

This argument is not reducible to the epistemic problem, although it is related to it. Epistemically imperfect judges make mistakes and may end up striking down statutes that do not violate people's rights and that advance the public good. But even epistemically perfect judges violate the public's right to political participation by striking down their (by hypothesis) ill-considered choices. Political participation, on this view, is an intrinsically valuable feature of life. Judicial interference with it harms people and violates their rights.

Consider various historical controversies—whether people have a right not to be enslaved; whether women have (or should have) the right to vote; whether women should have a right to obtain an abortion; whether gay people have or should have the right to marry people of the same sex. Judges were not the first people to argue for these rights and insist that the government should respect them. The idea that the people in question had rights that were being violated emerged from the general population—often led by intellectuals, or religious leaders, or politicians, or activists. Once the idea caught on, attempts were made to vindicate the rights—both in court and in the political arena. Thus, the picture of judges protecting rights antecedently determined in an early constitutional agreement is misleading. The correct picture is one in which judges play an ambiguous role in speeding up, slowing down, or modifying rights as they emerge in public discussion and political action.

Let us turn now to international human rights. The setting differs from that of domestic constitutional enforcement in many ways, but there are also some essential similarities. International human rights treaties identify rights that, in principle, supersede domestic political action. Thus, a domestic legislature is prohibited from passing laws that violate human rights. The public accordingly loses any meaningful opportunity to demand, debate about, and cause their representatives to pass legislation that infringes on any of the human rights. The damage to the right to political participation is, in this sense, similar to the damage done to the right to political participation at the domestic level through judicial enforcement of constitutional rights.

But international human rights, if enforced, can do more harm to the right to political participation than judicial enforcement of constitutional rights does. Within the United States, people can reassert their right to political participation as against judicial enforcement by agitating for a constitutional amendment, by exerting pressure on the judicial appointments process, and by pressuring the executive and legislature to challenge constitutional interpretations. In other countries, citizens can lobby the legislature to reverse judicial interpretations of the constitution. By contrast, there is no practical way to amend human rights treaties. As a matter of international law, a treaty can be amended only with the consent of all states—an unattainable threshold. In practice, states can, in effect, amend treaties by advancing their own interpretations and seeking consensus, but because this does not occur through any institutional process, it occurs haphazardly if at all. Therefore, if human rights treaties really did bind, they would deprive people of their right to political participation.

There are several responses to this argument. A first response is that a democratic judgment is made whether to enter into human rights treaties in the first place, and the right to political participation is vindicated in this way. This is a standard argument in constitutionalism, but it has few adherents today. The dead hand of the past will always constrain the present because of inertia and the costs of revisiting settled norms and procedures. But constitutions are especially problematic because they require supermajorities to amend, and so outdated constitutional norms can become deeply entrenched. The argument is still weaker for human rights treaties. While the U.S. Constitution was debated at great length at the time of the founding, I am unaware of any evidence that the human rights treaties were topics of meaningful public deliberation in the United States or any other democracy. They never had the political salience of a constitution, and were handled by governments in the course of other foreign policy duties.[12]

A second response by defenders of human rights treaties is that human rights treaties address only the worst types of rights violations, and the right to democratic participation does not encompass the right to debate whether people should be tortured or deprived of trials. This is an appealing argument but it is surely wrong. The rights not to be tortured and deprived of trials developed out of democratic deliberation; judicial intervention came later. In the United States, torture and denial of trials turned out to be topics of democratic deliberation in the first decade of the twenty-first century, when both of these instruments were used against Al Qaeda. Moreover, human rights treaties do not address only the worst type of rights violations. As we have seen, they encompass nearly all aspects of governance—health and pension policy, the rights of workers, schooling, welfare, the treatment of disabled people, race discrimination, and on and on. If all these topics are removed from democratic deliberation, then there will be little left for the people to discuss.[13]

The third response is that human rights treaties do not infringe on the right to political participation because governments can either denounce the treaties or (when the treaties lack a denunciation clause) refuse to recognize them as legally binding. Human rights treaties in this way differ from domestic constitutional law, which (at least in advanced countries) is enforced by powerful courts. But this response gives away the game. If states can evade human rights treaties, then they cannot have any positive value. Perhaps there is a subtle thread-the-needle argument that human rights treaties exert just enough force to cause states to improve governance but not so much as to interfere with democratic deliberation. But even if this argument were logically coherent, there is no evidence that human rights treaties play much role in political deliberation in Western countries.

But what of authoritarian countries? The fourth response is that human rights treaties do not interfere with political participation in democratic countries, where voters support the human rights embodied in the treaties or rights close enough to the rights in the treaties that any infringement on democratic deliberation is marginal. By contrast, the human rights treaties promote democratic participation in authoritarian countries, where democracy movements draw strength and inspiration from the treaties. Any modest harm to political participation in democratic countries is outweighed by the benefit in authoritarian countries, both from a global standpoint and from the standpoint of people living in democracies, who benefit from the spread of democracy around the world.

This is a powerful argument, but on inspection it fails as well. To begin, it is impossible to divide the world into (good) democratic states and (bad) authoritarian states. States fall along a continuum, and many states with authoritarian governments are responsive to the needs and interests of their populations. Consider China, which has greatly improved the standard of living of its population over the last 30 years—thus advancing their economic rights. A human rights treaty that required China to grant political rights might make it more difficult for the government to manage the economy. Political rights might lead to turmoil or civil war, or they might not—but the claim that this extremely difficult question can be settled by a human rights treaty containing some vague and mainly aspirational clauses drafted decades ago without the specific needs and conditions of China or any other particular country in mind is unpersuasive.

In sum, in countries on the democratic side of the spectrum, human rights treaties (to the extent they are enforceable) interfere with the right to political participation by taking numerous policy questions off the political agenda. This might be an acceptable price to pay if those treaties promoted democratic participation and other public goods in authoritarian states. As I have argued throughout this book, however, in practice the rights are too vague and too conflicting to bind authoritarian states; but even if they were not, then—and this is the dilemma I have repeatedly emphasized—there would be little reason to believe that the specific rights would promote the well-being of people in a diverse array of very different authoritarian countries, where the interests, values, and needs of the populations cannot be captured in a simple list of rights.

5.8. REPRISE

This chapter began with a discussion of why states lack incentives to comply with human rights treaties that do not merely ratify their existing policies, but concluded with normative arguments that explain why human rights treaties, even if complied with, would not advance the public good, while interfering with important political rights. The two ideas are connected. One reason governments do not pay much attention to human rights treaties is that they are responsible for advancing the public good, and the treaties themselves do not provide reliable guidance as to what promotes the public good. Moreover, governments that see themselves as obligated to respect the rights of citizens to engage in political participation cannot credibly shut down debate by citing treaty obligations that were agreed to decades earlier, usually without public debate, and that are in any event too vague and contestable to contradict positions advanced in the debate. Thus, even states with democratic traditions approach human rights treaties with caution—they are, and should be, reluctant about allowing human rights treaties to constrain domestic politics.

This logic also may explain why such states do not devote much effort to trying to compel foreign countries to comply with human rights treaties. The point is not (or not just) that voters care little about the well-being of foreigners. The danger is in the opposite direction: if voters care a great deal about the well-being of foreigners, but do not understand the interests of those foreigners and the conditions under which they live, then well-meaning attempts to enforce human rights treaties in those countries may, because of epistemic limits, lead to bad outcomes as well as interfere with the domestic right to political participation. The wisdom of the Westphalian system lay in the recognition that an excessive concern with the lives of foreigners, not too little concern, can be a major source of conflict in international relations.

CHAPTER SIX

Human Rights and War

HUMAN RIGHTS LAW is not specifically concerned with war and peace, but, as I noted in Chapter 1, there has long been a claim that if governments respected human rights, they would not go to war. This claim raises the question of whether it is true that human rights law contributes to peace. If it contributes to peace, or at least minimizes the risk of unjust wars, then human rights law could be defended even if it does not otherwise improve governments' treatment of their own citizens.

In this chapter, I criticize this claim. There is a complex and ambiguous relationship between respect for human rights and unwillingness to fight. The former does not necessarily lead to the latter.

6.1. THE HUMAN RIGHTS PEACE

The Universal Declaration of Human Rights was foremost a repudiation of fascism, which was blamed for World War II. Fascists believe that people should subordinate their interests to that of a large group—the state or a race—and that international relations is an arena of militarized conflict between different groups of people. The Nazis rejected human rights from the start, arguing that minorities should be excluded from national life, that independent state institutions like the judiciary must be subordinated to the party, and that people must yield to the will of the leader, who will act in the group interest but cannot be constrained by niceties like judicial process, multiparty democracy, and public criticism.

The Nazis' rejection of liberal democratic rights for German citizens was tied to their aggressive posture toward foreign countries, above all the rejection of the Treaty of Versailles—which meant the repudiation of reparations, the elimination of restrictions on the size of the army, and the recovery of German lands taken at the end of World War I. Hitler believed that all German-speaking populations should be united in a single state, and that Germans should colonize lands in eastern Europe and enslave their inhabitants. The Nazi Party employed paramilitaries, espoused military values, and attempted to unify Germans by demonizing foreign (as well as domestic) enemies. Thus, the Nazi government's military aggression against foreign countries starting in 1939 seemed to follow logically from its abrogation of civil and political rights starting in 1933. One interpretation of all this is that if Germany had somehow been forced to respect the rights of its own citizens, the Nazis would never have gained power and turned Germany against its neighbors. The Universal Declaration of Human Rights, and the human rights treaties that followed it, reflect this line of thinking.

But the causal mechanism that connects respect for human rights and aversion to war is obscure. Human rights treaties do not forbid countries to go to war. Although some human rights advocates argue that human rights treaties require countries to respect the human rights of enemy soldiers and civilians, most countries believe that the laws of war supersede human rights law in wartime. Thus, human rights law does not reduce the incentive to go to war by constraining how countries deploy weapons and tactics during war.

Perhaps human rights law encourages governments to take into account the interests and values of their citizens, and citizens generally oppose war. But that's not true, either. Ordinary people are often enthusiastic about war, or the benefits they believe a successfully prosecuted war will bring them. There is also a belief that human rights law encourages governments to refrain from violence, thus discouraging warfare, but liberal democracies go to war frequently—just not against each other.

This striking fact is the focus of the democratic peace literature, which provides a starting point for thinking about whether human rights law discourages states from going to war. Looking at a broad swath of history, from, say, 1800 to today, the only example of a major war between democracies was the War of 1812 between the United States and Great Britain, and even this example is not a strong one, as both countries were only partly democratic by modern standards. All other wars during this period took place between a democracy and a non-democracy, or two non-democracies. The two world wars featured authoritarian countries on both sides but democracies only on one side.

Today, there are no major interstate wars, but a number of flashpoints, and the pattern remains consistent. In Southeast Asia, China (authoritarian) has almost come to blows with Japan (democratic) and the Philippines (democratic). India (democratic) and Pakistan (authoritarian or at least quasi-authoritarian) remain enemies. Israel (democratic) and Iran (quasi-authoritarian) threaten to come to blows. There remain tensions between the United States (democratic) and North Korea (authoritarian). In the recent past, the United States fought with Afghanistan (authoritarian) and Iraq (authoritarian); Russia (authoritarian) fought Georgia (whose political system was ambiguous at the time). The Soviet Union (authoritarian) started numerous wars with other authoritarian states, like Afghanistan. Recent wars in Africa, including a conflict between Ethiopia and Eritrea, and conflicts involving numerous countries in Central Africa, featured authoritarian states fighting each other. In some cases, authoritarian policies seemed linked to aggression abroad, as in the case of Iraq's invasion of Iran and Kuwait, and Argentina's attempt to take the Falkland Islands from Great Britain. Meanwhile, despite all the tensions in Western Europe arising from the Eurozone crisis, the specter of war is as remote as ever. Latin American countries have fought each other in the past, but as the region democratizes, it has become more peaceful.

In fact, democracies are quite warlike—with non-democracies rather than with each other. Thus, respect for human rights in democracies does not lead to a generalized pacifism or aversion to war, or even to a preference (relative to authoritarian countries) for resolving conflicts using peaceful means. Of the 37 interstate wars (as defined by the Correlates of War project) between World War II and 2007, approximately 20 involved a democracy on one side, depending on how, exactly, one defines a democracy.

Moreover, the premise—that human rights treaties support the spread of democracy—is questionable. As I have argued, there is only weak evidence that human rights treaties have improved governments' respect for human rights. There is no evidence that human rights treaties have caused countries to become democracies. Indeed, the treaties themselves do not obligate countries to become democracies, though the ICCPR does create vague rights to political participation. The major cause of the spread of democracy since World War II has been the failure of many authoritarian systems to deliver economic growth to their populations, their propensity to entangle their countries in ruinous wars, and their many other unattractive features.

A more direct way to prevent nations from going to war with each other would be to try to force them to enter into treaties that prevent war, not treaties that require them to respect human rights. Of course, it is possible that human rights treaties over time encourage a more pacific disposition in populations, and there is no way to prove that this is not the case, though there is no evidence for it, either. It is also possible that human rights treaties, or the effort to spread human rights around the world, cause war. That is the topic of the next section.

6.2. HUMANITARIAN INTERVENTIONS

The idea that democracies are warlike (against non-democracies) rather than peaceful haunts a related debate about whether countries should engage in "humanitarian interventions"—military interventions to stop atrocities in other countries. The human rights treaties nowhere authorize countries to go to war against human rights abusers, and the UN charter bars use of military force that has not been authorized by the Security Council or that is not in self-defense. But in practice, human rights can play a role in instigating war. The use of military force remains the ultimate means for coercing states; and if human rights treaties are to be taken seriously, it may seem that military force will be needed to enforce them. States have agreed on a principle known as "responsibility to protect," which some have interpreted to authorize the use of military force against states that fail to respect the human rights of their populations. This principle is not a legal doctrine and does not supersede the UN charter as a matter of international law, but it exists as a hazy understanding among states.

States and commentators also frequently cite human rights when justifying war. The 1994 genocide in Rwanda helped promote this idea. With the benefit of hindsight, one can see clearly that foreign nations could have stopped the machete-wielding genocidaires if they had risked a military intervention. Regret at the failure to prevent hundreds of thousands of deaths, reinforced by the slow reaction to ethnic cleansing during the Yugoslav civil war of the same decade, finally led to a military intervention in Kosovo in 1999. After Serb forces began a campaign of ethnic cleansing against ethnic Albanians in the Serbian region of Kosovo, NATO, led by the United States, launched an air campaign that drove the Serbs out and secured autonomy for the region (which has since declared independence). Many complex motivations lay behind the war, as is always the case, but the humanitarian justification played a role, with supporters arguing that the war was necessary to prevent a genocide, or at least crimes against humanity, including massacres of civilians. An international commission later declared the war "illegal but legitimate," meaning that the humanitarian justification provided the moral basis for a war that was otherwise illegal because of the absence of Security Council authorization.

The U.S.-led war against Afghanistan and al Qaeda, which began in 2001, was also defended on humanitarian grounds. To be sure, the main justification was self-defense; but there was at the time a lot of now-forgotten talk about how a Western military intervention would not only free Afghanistan of the oppressive Taliban regime but pave the way to democracy and human rights. Much emphasis was put on the mistreatment of women by the Taliban, as well as its barbarous punishments of criminals and political dissenters. And while Afghanistan remains a backward place, gains for women were made, especially in areas controlled by the American-supported Afghan government, Kabul in particular.

Next came the 2003 war against Iraq. The Bush administration provided a number of justifications—the main one that of preemptive self-defense. The U.S. government believed, or persuaded itself into believing, or pretended to believe, that Iraq posed a military threat to the United States because it possessed weapons of mass destruction, which it might hand over to Al Qaeda. The U.S. government made sure to add that the Iraqi government practiced torture, political repression, and many other human rights abuses. Many people on the left in the United States supported the war on human rights grounds, and lent their voices to that of the Bush administration.

The 2011 military intervention in Libya also was justified, and probably to a large extent motivated, by humanitarian considerations. Western countries disliked Gaddafi and were glad to see him go. But the event that immediately led to the military intervention was his threat to massacre civilians in a rebel stronghold. The UN Security Council for the first time authorized a war on humanitarian grounds. The subsequent air war delivered a victory to the rebel forces.

Most recently, in September 2013 the United States almost launched an attack on Syria after the Syrian government massacred hundreds of civilians with chemical weapons. The U.S. government backed down after Russia offered to broker a deal in which the Assad government gave up its chemical weapons. The U.S. government had not intervened earlier in the years-long civil war despite many massacres using conventional weapons, and may have sought to deter chemical weapons use not because of their humanitarian cost but because of their potential for regional destabilization.

Political leaders have always justified wars by citing moral ideals, but it is fair to say that these recent wars have been more closely tied to human rights treaties—or at least the idea of human rights—than any others. This is not to say that human rights was the chief motivating factor in any of them. But they likely played a role in eliciting support from people who are otherwise skeptical of military action.

In this sense, human rights treaties have led to war, not ended it. And while the Kosovo and Libya interventions put an end to atrocities in the short term (the long-term future of human rights in Libya remains bleak), the Iraq intervention had only a modest impact, replacing a ruthless dictator with a somewhat less ruthless dictator, at great human cost. But could it be argued that these were short-term wars that made future wars less likely? And if so, was the net effect an overall reduction in human rights abuses?

It is always difficult to imagine a counterfactual, and so the discussion here is unavoidably speculative. Let us start with the best case for humanitarian intervention, which is the intervention in Kosovo and the former Yugoslavia more generally. That country broke up in 1991, as various ethnic enclaves sought independence from Serbia. Serbia reacted by attempting to expand the territory under its control. The most serious conflicts occurred in territories where people of different ethnic groups—Serbs, Croats, Muslim Bosnians, Slovenes, and others—lived together. Western intervention occurred at several stages, not just in Kosovo—most notably a bombing campaign in 1995, which led to a settlement in Bosnia-Herzegovina.

During the Yugoslavian civil war, a huge number of atrocities took place. Military and paramilitary forces massacred, raped, and starved civilians, and drove them from their homes. The military and diplomatic intervention by the West put an end to these atrocities. Moreover, pressure from the United States and the European Union helped introduce elections into these countries. After the wars ended, the former warring countries sought to join the European Union, and the EU set as a condition for entry that they uphold human rights and incorporate them into their legal systems. The militaristic and quasi-fascist elements in these countries lost their sway over public opinion and their influence in government. Although some problem spots remain—notably, Kosovo, whose viability as a state remains unclear, and Bosnia-Herzegovina, which remains unstable—the overall assessment must be that military as well as economic and diplomatic pressure not only improved human rights, but also created a group of (roughly) human-rights abiding countries that seem unlikely to go to war with each other or any other country anytime soon.

Iraq could have been seen as a test case for the theory that governments that fail to respect human rights internally pose a military threat to their neighbors. Under Saddam Hussein, who came to power in the 1970s, Iraq was a police state that suppressed political dissent with torture and other forms of abuse, and also engaged in war abroad. It used poison gas to suppress the Kurds in the north, and massacred rebellious Shiites in the south. It started a massive war with Iran in 1980, which ended only in 1988. And it invaded and conquered Kuwait in August of 1990, before being expelled by a U.S.-led multinational force in February of 1991. Not all states that abuse their populations start wars with other countries, but Iraq certainly did, and so a case could be made that a military intervention to remove Saddam Hussein and establish a democratic government that respects human rights would help pacify the region by reining in one of its most belligerent members.

From a humanitarian perspective, the war was a failure. Although Saddam Hussein was removed and his torture chambers were dismantled, the Kurds obtained autonomy in the north, and the long-oppressed Shiites came to power in the rest of the country, the political situation is still unstable. Iraq is not a democracy, nor does it respect human rights. Torture remains common, and civil strife has recently increased. The modest positive changes came at enormous cost—including civilian deaths, massive refugee movements, and general impoverishment.

The war also did not bring peace to the region. While Iraq has been sufficiently weakened that it will not be a threat to any other country in the near future, Iran has grown to fill the vacuum left by its traditional rival. Iraq's weakness also means that there will be a risk of instability in that area, especially around its borders near Syria, and indeed turmoil in Iraq may have contributed to the civil war in Syria that began in 2011. If the former Yugoslavia provides an ideal picture as to how human rights backed by military force can bring peace to a region, Iraq is the opposite.

The military attack on Libya was a purer example of humanitarian intervention than the involvement in either Yugoslavia or Iraq. Libya was a troublemaker—in the past it had supported international terrorism—but it had not gone to war with its neighbors in several decades. The military intervention in Libya stopped what would likely have been a massacre of civilians in the town of Benghazi. Gaddafi had announced "We'll clean Benghazi, all of Benghazi, of the deviants and of anyone who tries to harm our leader and our revolution. . . We will show no mercy to collaborators." But in the aftermath of the revolution, hundreds of independent militias were warring for control. It is too early to tell whether post-Gaddafi Libya will be an improvement, but it seems highly unlikely—given Libya's history and the norms of the region—that the military intervention will have brought peace to the region.

The near-intervention in Syria also seems like a purer case of humanitarian intervention—except that the U.S. government put the focus on chemical weapons. There is some reason to believe that the U.S. government's major concern was the risk that chemical weapons would reach non-state actors and potentially be used against Israel, and that the humanitarian implications were an afterthought. The Obama administration ultimately cited Syria's violation of a norm against the use of chemical weapons as the major justification for employing military force, but also emphasized the human suffering that those weapons caused. When Russia brokered a deal requiring Syria to give up its chemical weapons, the United

States backed away from its threat to attack, despite the continuing humanitarian crisis.

Meanwhile, military interventions were not launched in dozens of countries where human rights were routinely violated. In some cases, the countries were too powerful—North Korea and China. Sometimes, Western interests were too closely tied to those countries' prosperity (China again). Sometimes, the West had strong diplomatic, economic, or military reasons for cooperating with the countries—a point that could be made about almost the entire Middle East, or south Asia. In other cases, the West really had no interest in what was going on in those countries—much of sub-Saharan Africa. In short, humanitarian interventions will be launched only when it is relatively low-risk and the immediate gains are likely to be large (Libya), or where the humanitarian interest coincides with significant security and economic interests (Yugoslavia, Iraq).

A few observations are in order. First, the idea of humanitarian intervention remains highly controversial. Russia, China, and other major countries reject it. Its major champions are the United States and Great Britain. It is seen by Russia and China as an excuse for using military force against countries that the United States dislikes or distrusts, and ultimately—because it is based on an idea of human rights that they do not live up to—a threat to the legitimacy of their own systems.

Second, humanitarian intervention is not strongly supported by popular opinion, even in the West. The interventions in Kosovo and Libya, and the initial announcement of a planned intervention in Syria, were controversial in the United States. Americans usually demand a justification grounded in national security. Humanitarian goals can provide additional weight, as shown by the Bush administration's defense of the war in Iraq, but they cannot, as a practical matter, provide the sole justification for a war. This means that any war undertaken for humanitarian reasons will also reflect goals that are not humanitarian—goals relating to national security. It is in this sense that a law permitting humanitarian intervention may lead to a greater amount of warfare that is not necessarily morally justified.

Third, aside from the Kosovo intervention—which took place in a part of the world where European nations were willing to invest significant resources over the long term—the humanitarian interventions or quasi-humanitarian interventions either increased suffering among civilians or had no noticeable impact on the aggregate level of suffering. These results—along with the frequent cases where humanitarian interventions were not launched—tend to support the skepticism of those who see humanitarian intervention as a pretext for wars motivated by security concerns.

Fourth, the problem with humanitarian interventions is that they can further destabilize a society. Popular discussion often assumes that the interveners need merely to remove a dictator, and then democracy will bloom. But dictators often retain power by suppressing latent conflicts between different groups. When the dictator is removed, those conflicts are rekindled. This is what happened after Saddam Hussein and Muammar Gaddafi were deposed. And the risk that the elimination of Bashar Al-Assad would merely worsen the civil war in Syria has limited the attractiveness of military intervention there.

In sum, while the conventional wisdom is that humanitarian intervention or its threat may help force countries to comply with human rights treaties, thus promoting human rights, that same wisdom necessarily implies that human rights law, at least in the short term, makes war more likely than it would be under a system where Western countries left other countries alone. The argument that human rights law reduces war is an argument about the long run. If Western countries intervene often enough, advocates imply, then the threat of intervention will become credible, and so countries will stop violating human rights in order to avoid being invaded. The evidence does not support this argument, however. And the argument assumes that governments have more control over the level of human rights violations on their territory than they probably do.

6.3. THE LEAGUE OF DEMOCRACIES

A number of commentators and politicians have proposed that liberal democracies should form a "league" or "concert" that would put steady pressure on non-democracies to change their systems. In its most radical vision, the league would replace the United Nations Security Council, depriving China and Russia of the power to deny legal authority to military interventions against dictatorships. Just such a proposal was made by interventionists frustrated by China's and Russia's refusal to condemn the Syrian government's massacres of civilians in the Syrian civil war.

The League of Democracies is a radical idea from the standpoint of international law, since it would exist in defiance of many countries, including several of the most powerful. It is driven by frustration with a state of affairs in which nearly all countries give their consent to human rights treaties but many countries refuse to comply with them, and nearly all countries refuse to enforce them against each other. But if one accepts human rights treaties as law, the League of Democracies is a logical implication of it. The problem is enforcement, and since only liberal democracies take human rights seriously, only liberal democracies can be depended on to enforce them.

The League of Democracies is driven by a vision of a world in which all countries respect human rights and are at peace with each other. It is an appealing vision, but the problem is getting from here to there. Countries excluded from the League of Democracies will be more reluctant than ever to cooperate with members in areas such as trade and security where there are shared interests. Thus, a League of Democracies, by further institutionalizing and promoting the idea that states that violate human rights lack legitimacy, would contribute to international polarization and disorder, and for the sake of a utopian goal—a world of human rights respecting and peaceful states—that is unlikely to be realized.

CHAPTER SEVEN

A Fresh Start
Human Rights and Development

7.1. THREE DEAD ENDS

Can human rights law be saved? I briefly address here, partly by way of summary, three frequently heard proposals for improving human rights law, and explain why they lead to dead ends.

Give priority to a narrow set of rights. A recurrent theme among scholars who worry that human rights law is ineffective or less effective than it should be is that there are too many rights. There are different reasons for thinking that this is a problem. Some rights may seem frivolous and thus throw the enterprise into disrepute. A more serious objection—which I have emphasized in this book— is that when many rights exist, a state can justify its failure to respect one right by insisting that it has exhausted financial and political resources trying to comply with other rights—which makes it difficult either to criticize states for violating rights or to enforce rights.

The solution is to start over again by identifying a small number of fundamental rights, and giving them priority over all the other rights. We can *expect* states to comply with all of the rights, but *demand* them to comply with the fundamental rights. Many scholars have, in various ways, taken this position, and the rights-enforcing countries, in practice, focus on a small number of rights—typically political freedoms and protections from criminal law enforcement—and give less emphasis to others.

This approach is a dead end because the relevant rights-enforcers cannot agree that a specific subset of rights are fundamental while the others are not. Moreover, countries need to be able to allocate resources to human interests that may seem less urgent than others (for example, entertainment as opposed to bodily integrity) when the marginal dollar devoted to the urgent interests yields trivial gains in human well-being. The reason that human rights have proliferated is precisely that countries disagree on priorities and all countries recognize a huge number of diverse human interests, large and small, that should be a matter of concern for government policy.

Use a margin of appreciation. Another concern is that human rights law is too rigid. It fails to take account of the different circumstances that states face. Many states disregard human rights law because it imposes unrealistic demands on them.

A solution might be to more clearly recognize a "margin of appreciation" for human rights law or for international law generally. On this view, states would have some (but not complete) discretion in implementing their obligations under international human rights law. In doctrinal terms, courts and other enforcers would give some deference to states when they argue that their activities do not violate human rights law. This approach seems to work well in some national legal systems, as well as in the European Human Rights domain, where the ECHR has frequently invoked the margin of appreciation doctrine to justify a ruling in favor of a state.

This solution also will go nowhere. Part of the problem is the sheer nebulousness of the margin of appreciation doctrine, which the ECHR appears to invoke either selectively or to mop up outliers. It is far from clear what it means for a court to give some but not too much deference. It may be that states already effectively recognize a margin of appreciation and that is why they enforce human rights law so poorly against other countries. But on this view, the margin of appreciation is the problem, not the solution. The margin of appreciation approach is plausible only if it can be implemented by a centralized body like the ECHR, which enjoys the support of the states. Because no such international institution exists, this is another dead end.

Institutionalize. Many human rights advocates understand that human rights treaties are not self-enforcing, that relying on biased and interested states to enforce them may be self-defeating, and that human rights enforcement requires the involvement of independent international institutions. As we have seen, this recognition has produced an enormous menagerie of committees, councils, commissions, offices, and courts, with complexly overlapping jurisdictions and varying capacities—nearly all undermined by resource starvation or legal restrictions on their authority.

A recurrent proposal for improving human rights enforcement is to strengthen these institutions—to give them power, support, resources, and whatever else they need. A group of prominent human rights advocates—including a former UN High Commissioner of Human Rights and a current president of the International Criminal Tribunal for the Former Yugoslavia—have proposed a World Court for Human Rights, which would have the authority to enforce human rights law around the globe.

This proposal is also a dead end. International organizations depend for their finances, power, and existence on the support and tolerance of states, and states do not want to improve enforcement of human rights by giving international organizations more power. The problem, as I have argued, is not so much that states don't care about human rights, but that they will not grant discretion to a body consisting mostly of foreigners who lack knowledge, sympathy, and sophistication about the problems that they face.

I do not believe that human rights law will end with a bang. States are not going to withdraw from human rights treaties, for example, or denounce human rights in public statements. Instead, the idea of a rigid legal framework will gradually dissolve into a soup of competing and unresolvable claims about which interests deserve human rights protections, which interests do not, and how much weight should be placed on each. That, of course, is what I have already described, but the process is sufficiently murky and unfinished that it seems safest to say that human rights law is experiencing a twilight existence that may linger for quite a while.

7.2. THE WHITE MAN'S BURDEN

"The White Man's Burden" is the sardonic title of an influential book on foreign aid by William Easterly, and the title of the poem by Rudyard Kipling, an apologist for British imperialism.[1] Easterly argues that much of the foreign aid establishment is in the grip of an ideology that is a softer-edge version of the civilizing mission of nineteenth-century imperialists. Westerners no longer believe that white people are superior to other people on racial grounds, but they do believe that regulated markets, the rule of law, and liberal democracy are superior to the systems that prevail in non-Western countries, and they have tried to implement those systems in the developing world. Easterly himself does not oppose regulated markets and liberal democracy, nor does he oppose foreign aid. He instead attacks the ideology of the "Planners"—people who believe that the West can impose from above a political and economic blueprint that will advance well-being in other countries. Anecdotal and statistical evidence show that while narrow, carefully thought-through, and rigorously implemented measures (for example, certain vaccination campaigns) can improve the lives of poor people, most aid programs are comprehensive, ambitious, utopian failures.

Over many decades, Western countries contributed trillions of dollars of aid to developing countries. The aid has taken many different forms: unrestricted cash, loans at below-market interest rates, cash that must be used to buy Western products, in-kind projects like dams and plants, technical assistance, education, training, and "rule-of-law" projects designed to improve the quality of legal institutions. For a while, the "Washington consensus" imposed cookie-cutter market-based prescriptions on countries that needed to borrow money. The consensus now among economists is that these efforts have failed. The reasons are varied. Giving cash and loans to a government to build projects like power plants will not help the country if government officials pocket the money or skim off a large share, and give contracts to cronies who lack the motive and ability to implement the projects. Directly building a power plant for a country will not help it if the country lacks the legal infrastructure to enforce contracts and protect property rights, for without that infrastructure the owners of the power plant cannot earn revenues sufficient to cover the cost of maintenance and other inputs. Providing experts to improve the legal infrastructure of the country will not help if local judges refuse to enforce the new laws because of corruption or tradition or incompetence. Training judges will not help if the judges are controlled by corrupt government officials. Pressuring governments to combat corruption will not help if payoffs to mob bosses, clan chiefs, or warlords are needed to maintain social order. Demanding that aid recipients use money in ways that donors believe proper and recipients believe unnecessary can engender suspicion and evasion of the conditions of the donations. The Washington consensus failed because economic reform requires the consent of the public, and populations resented the imposition of harsh policies by foreigners, policies that were not always wise on their own terms.

In the words of two highly regarded development economists:

> Very bad policies are sometimes born out of the best of intentions, because of a misreading of what the real problem is: Public school systems fail the majority because everyone believes that only the elite can learn. Nurses never come to work because no one tried to make sure that there was demand for their services and because of unrealistic expectations about what they can do. Poor people have no safe place to save because the regulatory standards that governments sets for institutions that are allowed to legally accept savings are absurdly high.[2]

The difficulty, they continue, is that the problems that governments and donors seek to solve are complicated and so are the solutions.

International human rights law is another element in the Plan of the Planners, reflecting the same basic civilizing ideology combined with the same top-down mode of implementation, pursued in the same crude manner. But human rights law has its distinctive features as well. Because it is law, it requires the consent of states, creating an illusion of symmetry and even-handedness that is absent from foreign aid. Hence the insistence, wholly absent from discussions about foreign aid, that Western countries are just as subject to international human rights law as other countries are. In practice, as we have seen, international human rights law does not require Western countries to change their behavior, while (in principle) it requires massive changes in the behavior of most non-Western countries. Because human rights law is law, it is the stick, corresponding to the carrot of foreign aid. Both foreign aid and human rights enforcement can be corrupted or undermined because Western countries have strategic interests that are not always aligned with the missions of those institutions. But the major problem, in both cases, is that both systems cannot handle the variation and complexity of non-Western countries.

Development economics has gone some distance to curing itself of this failing. While Planners still exist, the best development scholars have been experimenting furiously with different ways of improving lives of people living in foreign countries. Rigorous statistical methods are increasingly used, and in recent years economists have implemented a range of randomized controlled trials. Expectations have been ratcheted down; the goal is no longer to convert poor societies into rich societies, or even to create market institutions and eliminate corruption; it is to help a school encourage children to read in one village, or to simplify lending markets in another.

By contrast, human rights law has addressed the problems of variation and complexity by weaving between two inconsistent paths: insisting that all countries at least comply with a "core" group of narrow (mainly political) rights, and rationalizing diverse government behaviors through human rights hypertrophy. The type of academic rigor in development economics is absent from human rights law, where rule naiveté continues to prevail. Until recently, hardly anyone bothered to use rigorous scientific methods to test the effect of human rights treaties and institutions. Even today, empirical research is vanishingly rare. In the legal literature, a hundred papers parsing human rights doctrine to ever finer degrees are written for every paper that takes an empirical approach. Lawyers mainly read and discuss judicial opinions—which hardly affect anyone at all—while ignoring the actual behavior of governments, NGOs, and individuals.

There are, thus, parallels between human rights and foreign aid. Both approaches suffer from a historical failure to grapple with the huge variation among states and their extreme complexity—though the scholarship on aid is significantly more sophisticated and attuned to these problems than the scholarship on human rights. But today human rights law alone suffers from the problem of rule naiveté—the misconception that the public good for any country can be described in the form of simple rules. When foreign aid donors try to help a country, they recognize that the goal is to improve the well-being of the recipients—better health, greater economic activity, higher levels of literacy, and so on. When human rights advocates try to help a county, their goal is to bring the country into compliance with rules— fewer detentions, less torture, more free speech—which do not necessarily advance the well-being of the citizens in the target country. It is this narrowness and indirectness that makes human rights law more troublesome than foreign aid.

Could one abandon human rights law without giving up on efforts to improve the well-being of people who live in foreign countries, especially those who live under despotic or poorly functioning governments? A starting point is the observation that people in wealthy countries seem to take at least some interest in the well-being of people in poor countries. This can be seen most obviously when natural disasters strike and wealthy countries send aid, as they recently did to Haiti and the Philippines. All of the rich countries maintain foreign aid budgets as well, and much (but not all) of the money in these budgets is used to fund development projects and supply medical care. The rich world is not willing to make great sacrifices for people in poor countries, but it is willing to devote some resources to helping them.

One can similarly see human rights as a development project, an effort by the West to help people in non-Western countries by encouraging governments in those countries to respect human rights.

The argument takes the form of a simple syllogism: governments in poor countries generally do not respect human rights; human rights are good; therefore, rich countries can help people in poor countries by encouraging their governments to respect human rights.

Amartya Sen is well known for making this argument.[3] A development economist, he frequently confronted an old-fashioned belief from the 1960s and 1970s that a poor country could enjoy economic growth or a democratic government, but not both. Most development economists argued that the best hope for poor countries was first to industrialize; and then, once a certain level of wealth was achieved, to democratize and start respecting human rights. The development success stories of the day, including South Korea and Taiwan, fit this model. But Sen argued that human rights law advances economic growth and is also a worthy end in itself.

But Sen just exchanged one caricature for another. He was right that there is no rule that poor democracies cannot develop; but neither is there any reason to believe that a country where human rights are respected will grow faster than a country where they are not respected. Political liberty can advance economic growth by giving the people a means of punishing governments that fail to provide for them, but it also can interfere with economic growth by generating popular government policies that undermine growth.

There is a better way to think about development and human rights. Rather than devise general rules or theoretical approaches, consider each country on its own terms. All countries are different and all counties have different needs. It might make more sense for Western donors to help a country build a reliable road system than to force it to abolish torture. It may well be easy to build the road using donors' funds and local labor. Once built, the road may spur economic development, and even lead to greater political liberty by allowing people to travel to voting booths and enabling candidates to stump about the country. Meanwhile, if torture is an entrenched practice of the police force, no amount of aid for retraining the police and improving the judicial system will make any difference. If the goal is to help people in poor countries, and limited funds are available, then those funds should be used in ways that do the most good, not to compel the country to submit to an abstract formulation of human rights that Westerners imagine are right for everyone in the world.

As noted earlier, development aid does not always work. Indeed, there is a lively debate about whether it *ever* works. And so one response to my argument is that if development aid does not work, then using resources to encourage human rights is a better way to advance the well-being of people in poor countries. This response forces us to confront an unpleasant reality. There is very little that the West can do for poor countries. It turns out that foreign countries really are foreign. It is hard for us to understand their peoples, customs, institutions, and pathologies. It is often hard to tell whether efforts to help those countries improve the well-being of people or just create new problems.

Even very simple and apparently unaggressive ways of helping poor countries—for example, agreeing to trade with them—can disrupt traditions, destroy institutions, and play havoc with the political order. Similarly, giving money to governments can lead to kleptocracy, or cause civil wars, as people form insurgencies in the hope of gaining access to the foreign treasure. Giving money to local NGOs can disrupt political patterns, foment dissent, and cause disorder. Lending money for the construction of power plants can cause environmental damage, harm traditional forms of economic subsistence, and also cause political problems.

Development economists talk of the "resource curse," and some hypothesize that countries with valuable natural resources can suffer because the exploitation of those resources leads to political instability rather than riches for all. Some commentators have speculated that the promise of foreign aid bounty is itself a kind of resource curse, and can lead to the same pathologies that abundant natural resources do.

A recent literature in development economics suggests that economic growth is to a large extent a function of events from the distant past, even the Neolithic era. Geography, climate, population movements, cultural norms, technology advantages, wealth inequalities, and institutional developments from centuries in the past may lead to modern institutions, habits, norms, and beliefs that promote or thwart economic growth today.[4] The implications of this literature for human rights has not yet been examined, but one possibility is that human rights outcomes may be mostly determined by history, contingent pathways to development, population movements, and the like, in which case modern efforts to cooperate through international law are likely to affect behavior little or not at all.

If it is possible for Western countries to help poor countries to develop, foreign donors, whether rich countries, individuals, or institutions, cannot rely on formulas but must experiment and adjust in light of experience. Maybe supplying malaria nets is the best way to help country X but not apparently similar country Y. Maybe supplying malaria nets is helpful in country X at first, but then stops being helpful. A famous foreign aid story tells of how recipients of free mosquito nets distributed by foreign donors to combat malaria used them instead for fishing lines and fencing for gardens.

Now consider human rights. Will foreign efforts to encourage or coerce a developing country to allow greater political dissent help or hurt? The answer is that *it depends*. Sometimes it will help; sometimes it will hurt. Knowing when it will help and when it will hurt is difficult, and requires sensitivity to local conditions. Pressuring an authoritarian state to liberalize may cause a backlash, or it may encourage local dissenters. Whatever the case, it is clear that no algorithm will disclose what the right thing to do is.

A better way forward is to do without algorithms. A wealthy state, international NGO, or other group can start by identifying the states that are most in need of help. These are not necessarily the states that violate human rights the most; they may just be the states that are very poor. The next question is whether the misery of the population can be attributed to poor choices by the government, or instead is the result of deeper factors—cultural, demographic, political. In many countries, the problem is not that the government violates human rights; it is that the government is too weak to keep order because the population is divided into hostile tribes, clans, and other groups. In such countries, there may be little that the West can do to help.

What I am arguing for, then, is recognition that wealthy countries can and should provide foreign aid to developing countries, and use tools of coercion if necessary, based on a rough sense of whether the aid or coercion will enhance the well-being of the population, and of whether the government in the donee country will cooperate or undermine these efforts. Such a judgment should be made independently of whether the government complies with human rights treaties. This will mean abandoning the human rights treaties' greatest potential advantage—which is to provide a method for different countries to coordinate development assistance (as well as means of pressure) by creating a common set of priorities. But as I have explained, this effort never succeeded in the first place because it was never possible to agree on what the common set of priorities was, nor the extent to which bribing or forcing a country to comply with the treaties would actually benefit the population.

With the benefit of hindsight, we can see that the human rights treaties were not so much an act of idealism as an act of hubris, with more than a passing resemblance to the civilizing efforts undertaken by governments and missionary groups in the nineteenth century, which did little good for native populations while entangling European powers in the affairs of countries they did not understand. A more humble approach is long overdue.

Acknowledgments

...

I received valuable comments from workshop participants at Princeton, Northwestern, and the University of Chicago. I thank Daniel Abebe, Adam Chilton, Jack Goldsmith, Aziz Huq, Josh Kleinfeld, Nethanel Lipshitz, Ryan Long, Martha Nussbaum, Jide Nzelibe, and Adrian Vermeule for comments on several chapters; Mila Versteeg for her careful and very helpful comments on the entire manuscript; Geof Stone for his very helpful comments on the manuscript as well as his superb editing; and David McBride, my editor at Oxford, for his helpful suggestions. I also thank Matthew Brincks, Siobhan Fabio, Lea Madry, John Moynihan, Ellie Norton, Jullia Park, and Olga Vinogradova for helpful research assistance.

Appendix: List of Rights

. . .

The table below lists the rights that are recognized in the major human rights treaties. The table should not be taken literally. A right is not a natural kind and can be described at higher or lower levels of generality. For example, the right to privacy in communications could be redescribed as a right to privacy in the mails, a right to privacy in phone communications, a right to privacy in email communications, a right to equal privacy rights, and so on; or it could be combined with the right to privacy in the home as a single general "right to privacy." Little weight should be placed on the exact number of rights; the number will always be controversial. What one should take away from the table is the huge scope of human activity that the rights cover.

International Convention on the Elimination of All Forms of Racial Discrimination (ICERD)

Equality regardless of race, color, descent, or national or ethnic origin
    Right to equal treatment before tribunals
    Right to security of person
    Right to effective protection and remedies
    Political rights

(Continued)

(Continued)

International Convention on the Elimination of All Forms of Racial Discrimination (ICERD)

Civil rights
Right to freedom of movement and residence
Right to leave any country and return to one's own
Right to nationality
Right to marriage and choice of spouse
Right to own property
Right to inherit
Right to freedom of thought, conscience, and religion
Right to freedom of opinion and expression
Right to freedom of peaceful assembly and association
Economic, social, and cultural rights
Right to form and join trade unions
Right to housing
Right to public health, medical care, social security, and social services
Right to education and training
Right to equal participation in cultural activities
Right of access to any public place or service
Freedom from racial segregation
Prohibition of racist propaganda and organizations

International Covenant on Civil and Political Rights (ICCPR)

Right of self-determination
Freedom to dispose of own wealth and resources
No deprivation of own means of subsistence
Inherent right to life
Restrictions and rights for anyone sentenced to death
Freedom of expression
General gender equality clause
Freedom of thought, conscience, and religion
Prohibition of arbitrary arrest and detention
Right to assembly
Right to privacy of the home
Right to association
Right to privacy of communication

(Continued)

(Continued)

International Covenant on Civil and Political Rights (ICCPR)

Freedom of movement
Equal enjoyment of civil and political rights regardless of gender
Right of access to court and tribunals (habeas corpus)
Prohibition of torture
Right to vote
Prohibition of ex post facto laws
Freedom to choose residence
Freedom to leave any country
Rights of lawful alien in face of expulsion
Right not to be expelled from home territory
Equality regardless of race
Right to present a defense
Right to form trade unions
Right to counsel
Right to public trial
Right to review by a higher tribunal
Presumption of innocence until proven guilty
Rights regarding trial preparation
Freedom from forced testimony or confession of guilt
Right to establish a family
Prohibition of slavery
Freedom from forced labor
Right to liberty and security of person
Rights of arrested person
Rights for children
Right to a remedy when rights are violated
Right to personal privacy
Prohibition of double jeopardy
Equality regardless of belief/philosophy
Right to remain silent
Right to a timely trial
Equality regardless of political opinion
Right to an interpreter
Equality regardless of language
Right to 'fair trial'
Right to work for the government

(Continued)

(Continued)

International Covenant on Civil and Political Rights (ICCPR)

Right to privacy of family life
Minority cultural rights
Right to protection of one's reputation or honor
Equality husband and wife within the family
Right to appeal to higher court
Equality regardless of economic status
Equality regardless of nationality
Rights for prisoners

International Covenant on Economic, Social and Cultural Rights (ICESCR)

Right of self-determination
General gender equality clause
Right to education
Right to a fair wage
Right to work
Right to highest mental and physical health
Equality in employment promotion
Right to form and join trade unions
Right to establish a family
Right to social security
Right to protection and assistance to the family
Right to culture
Artistic freedom
Right to rest and leisure
Right to housing
Right to favorable working conditions
Right to protection of intellectual property
Right to strike
Right to adequate standard of living
Women's empowerment in labor relations
Right to maternity leave
Prohibition of child labor
Right to food
Right to take part in cultural life
Right to enjoy scientific progress

(Continued)

(Continued)

Convention on the Elimination of all Forms of Discrimination Against Women (CEDAW)

Legislative equality regardless of gender
Equality for women in political and public life
Prohibition of trafficking and prostitution of women
Equality of the husband and wife in marriage and family relations
    Same right to enter into marriage
    Same right to freedom in choosing a spouse and entering into marriage
    Same rights and responsibilities
    Same rights with regards to their children
    Same personal rights as husband and wife
    Same rights with regards to property
Right to acquire, change, or retain nationality
Equality for women in the field of education
Equality for women in the field of employment
    Right to safe working conditions
    Right to social security
    Women's empowerment in labor relations
    Right to maternity leave
    Right to social services such as child-care facilities
    Special protection during pregnancy
Equality for women in the field of health care
Equality for women in rural areas
    Right to participate in development planning
    Right to health care
    Right to benefit from social security programs
    Right to training and education
    Right to self-help groups and co-operatives
    Right to participate in community activities
    Right to adequate living conditions

Convention Against Torture, and Other Cruel, Inhuman or Degrading Treatment or Punishment (CAT)

Prohibition of torture
Protection from extradition to another State where danger of torture exists
Rights while in custody for alleged offense
    Right to communicate with appropriate representative

(Continued)

(Continued)

Convention Against Torture, and Other Cruel, Inhuman or Degrading Treatment or Punishment (CAT)

Right to have national State immediately notified of the custody
Fair treatment in proceedings
Prompt and impartial investigation of an alleged act of torture
Rights for complainants and victims of torture
Right to complain about act of torture
Right to protection
Right to fair and adequate compensation
Prohibition regarding statements made as a result of torture
Prohibition of other acts of cruel, inhuman, or degrading treatment or punishment

---

Convention on the Rights of the Child (CRC)

Rights for Children
Inherent right to life
Right to a name and nationality
Right to know and be cared for by parents
Right to preservation of identity
No separation from parents against child's will
Protection from illicit transfer abroad and non-return
Freedom of expression
Freedom of thought, conscience, and religion
Freedom of association and of peaceful assembly
Right to privacy
Freedom from attacks on honor and reputation
Access to mass media information and materials
Right to physical and mental protection
Right to humanitarian assistance
Right to good health
Right to social security
Right to an adequate standard of living
Right to education
Right to rest and leisure
Protection from harmful employment
Protection from illicit use of drugs
Protection from use of children in drug trafficking

(Continued)

(Continued)

Convention on the Rights of the Child (CRC)

    Protection from sexual exploitation and sexual abuse
    Protection from torture and other cruel, inhuman or degrading treatment and punishment
    Protection from abduction, sale, and trafficking
    Protection from all other forms of exploitation
    Protection from capital punishment and life imprisonment
    Protection of children in armed conflicts
Prohibition of child labor
Best interests of the child as the primary consideration
Rights and duties of parents are respected
Rights for disabled children
Rights for minority children to enjoy own culture
Rights of children deprived of liberty
Rights of children accused of infringing penal law

Second Optional Protocol to the International Covenant on Civil and Political Rights (ICCPR-OP2)

No execution
Prohibition of death penalty

International Convention on the Protection of the Rights of All Migrant Workers and Members of their Families (CMC)

Equality for all migrant workers and their families
    Free to leave any State
    Right to enter and remain in their State of origin
    Right to life
    Freedom from torture and cruel, inhuman, or degrading treatment/punishment
    Freedom from slavery
    Freedom from forced labor
    Right to freedom of thought, conscience, and religion
    Right to opinions
    Right to freedom of expression
    Right to privacy
    Freedom from unlawful attacks on honor and reputation
    Freedom from arbitrary deprivation of property

(Continued)

(Continued)

International Convention on the Protection of the Rights of All Migrant Workers and Members of their Families (CMC)

Right to liberty and security of person
Right to protection
Freedom from arbitrary arrest or detention
Equal rights as nationals
Freedom from confiscation or destroying of legal documents
Freedom from collective expulsion
Right to protection and assistance by their State of origin
Right to recognition as a person
Rights regarding employment
    Equal treatment and benefits as nationals
    Rights to form or join trade unions
    Rights to social security
    Right freely to choose remunerated activity
Rights to medical care
Rights of child
    Right to a name, registration of birth, and a nationality
    Right to education
    Right to learn mother tongue and culture
Right to a cultural identity
Rights upon termination of stay
Right to be informed
Right to liberty of movement
Freedom to choose residence
Right to participate in public affairs of State of origin
Right to political rights in State of employment, if granted
Equal treatment with nationals of State of employment
Protection of unity of family
Equality in accessing education
Equality in accessing social and health services
Equality in participating in cultural life
Rights regarding taxes
Rights for family of deceased migrant worked or dissolution of marriage
Rights for arrested migrant workers and their families
    Right to be informed about arrest in own language
    Right to trial or release

(Continued)

(Continued)

---

*International Convention on the Protection of the Rights of All Migrant Workers
and Members of their Families (CMC)*

Own State shall be notified of the detention
Right to communicate and meet with authorities in the own State
Right to a court trial
Victims of unlawful arrest or detention have the right to compensation
Right to be treated with humanity
Equal rights as nationals
Rights for accused migrant workers and their families
  Right to be separated from convicted persons
  Rights for juvenile persons to be separated from adults
  Right to be presumed innocent until proven guilty
  Rights in the determination of criminal charges
  Right to be reviewed by a higher tribunal
Freedom from imprisonment for failing to fulfill a contractual obligation
Rights for expelled migrant workers and their families
Rights for frontier workers
Rights for seasonal workers
Rights for itinerant workers
Rights for project-tied workers
Rights for specified-employment workers
Rights for self-employment workers
Rights regarding international migration
  Rights to sound, equitable, humane, and lawful conditions
  Rights to services to deal with questions

---

*Optional Protocol to the Convention on the Rights of the Child on the
Involvement of Children in Armed Conflict (CRC-OP (Armed Conflict))*

Prohibition of armed forces members aged <18 from taking direct part in
hostilities
Prohibition of children aged <18 from compulsory recruitment into armed
forces
Special protection for persons aged <18
Armed groups prohibited from recruiting or using in hostilities persons
aged <18
Rights of the child in more protective laws are unaffected
Assistance to victims of acts contrary to this Protocol

(Continued)

(Continued)

Optional Protocol to the Convention on the Rights of the Child on the Sale of Children, Child Prostitution and Child Pornography (CRC-OP (Sale of Children/Prostitution/Pornography))

Prohibition of the sale of children, child prostitution, and child pornography
Rights of child victims
    Right to recognition of vulnerability
    Right to adapted procedures to address special needs
    Right to be informed of the proceedings and the disposition
    Right to have views, needs, and concerns presented and considered
    Right to support services
    Right to privacy and identity
    Right to safety
    Right to avoid unnecessary delay in the proceedings
    Assistance in recovery
    Access to procedures to seek compensation for damages
Best interests of the child is the primary consideration
Rights of the child in more protective laws are unaffected

Convention on the Rights of Persons with Disabilities (CRPD)

Rights for the disabled
    Equal protection and benefit of the law
    Recognition of women and girls with disabilities
    Recognition of children with disabilities
    Access to public services facilities
    Right to life
    Right to protection in situations of risk
    Access to justice
    Right to liberty and security
    Freedom from torture or cruel, inhuman, or degrading treatment/punishment
    Freedom from exploitation, violence, and abuse
    Right to respect for physical and mental integrity
    Right to liberty of movement and nationality
    Right to live independently
    Right to be included in the community
    Right to personal mobility

(Continued)

(Continued)

Convention on the Rights of Persons with Disabilities (CRPD)

Freedom of expression and opinion
Access to information
Right to privacy
Respect for home and the family
Right to education
Right to good health
Access to habilitation and rehabilitation services and programs
Right to work
Right to an adequate standard of living
Right to social protection
Freedom to participate in political and public life
Freedom to participate in cultural life, recreation, leisure, and sport

---

International Convention for the Protection of All Persons from Enforced Disappearance (ICCPED)

Protection from enforced disappearance
Rights for individual who alleges enforced disappearance
    Right to report facts to authorities
    Right to protection
Protection from extradition to another State where danger of enforced disappearance exists
No secret detention
Right to information on deprivation of liberty
Right to privacy of personal information
Rights for victims of enforced disappearance
    Right to the truth
    Right to reparation and compensation
Right to form and participate in organizations that address enforced disappearance

---

Notes

. . .

INTRODUCTION

1. Joseph Raz, Human Rights Without Foundations 321, in The Philosophy of International Law (Samantha Besson & John Tasioulas eds., Oxford Univ. Press 2010).

2. David L. Cingranelli & David L. Richards, The Cingranelli and Richards (CIRI) Human Rights Data Project, 32 Hum. Rts. Q. 401 (2010); the data are available at http://humanrightsdata.blogspot.com/.

3. Arch Puddington, Freedom in the World 2013: Democratic Break-throughs in the Balance, at 4 http://www.freedomhouse.org/sites/default/files/FIW%202013%20Booklet_0.pdf. Freedom House is associated with conservative figures in the American political establishment, and therefore its scoring is sometimes treated as suspect.

CHAPTER ONE

1. Lynn A. Hunt, Inventing Human Rights: A History (W. W. Norton & Co. 2007).

CHAPTER TWO

1. Liora Lazarus, The Right to Security—Securing Rights or Stabilizing Rights, in Examining Critical Perspectives on Human Rights (R. Dickinson et al., eds., Cambridge Univ. Press 2012).

2. Navanethem Pillay, United Nations Human Rights, Strengthening the United Nations Human Rights Treaty Body System 94 (2012).

3. Yuval Shany, The Effectiveness of the Human Rights Committee and the Treaty Body Reform, 20 (Hebrew Univ. Fac. of Law, Int'l Law F., Research Paper No. 02-13, 2013).

4. Id. at 21.

5. Freedom House, The UN Human Rights Council Report Card: 2009-2010, at 2 (2010).

6. Id.

7. Andreas von Staden, Shaping Human Policy in Liberal Democracies: Assessing and Explaining Compliance with the Judgments of the European Court of Human Rights 133 (Princeton U. 2009); Courtney Hillebrecht, From Paper Tigers to Engines of Change: The Effect of Regional Human Rights Courts on Domestic Practice and Politics 85 (May 10, 2010) (unpublished Ph.D. dissertation, University of Wisconsin-Madison).

8. Freedom House, Country Ratings and Status, http://www.freedomhouse.org/report-types/freedom-world.

9. Human Rights Watch, World Report 2013, Russia, http://www.hrw.org/world-report/2013/country-chapters/russia.

CHAPTER THREE

1. See Richard Nielsen & Beth A. Simmons, Rewards for Ratification: Payoffs for Participating in the International Human Rights Regime? (2013) (unpublished manuscript, available at http://www.mit.edu/~rnielsen/Rewards%20for%20Ratification_18jan2014.pdf). There were small positive results in some specifications, but they are overwhelmed by the number of null results.

2. Andrew Moravcsik, The Origins of Human Rights Regimes: Democratic Delegation in Postwar Europe, 54 Int'l Org. 217 (2000).

3. Oona A. Hathaway, Why Do Countries Commit to Human Rights Treaties?, 51 J. Conflict Resol. 588 (2007); Beth Simmons, Mobilizing for Human Rights: International Law in Domestic Politics (Cambridge Univ. Press 2009).

CHAPTER FOUR

1. Beth A. Simmons, Mobilizing for Human Rights: International Law in Domestic Politics 236-53 (2009).

2. Zachary Elkins et al., Getting to Rights: Treaty Ratification, Constitutional Convergence, and Human Rights Practice, 54 Harv. Int'l L.J. 61 (2013); Mila Versteeg, Substitutes or Duplicates? The Relationship Between International and National Bills of Rights, unpublished manuscript (2013) (finding limited evidence).

3. See David S. Law & Mila Versteeg, Sham Constitutions, 101 Calif. L. Rev. 863 (2013). See also Christian Bjørnskov & Jaco Mchangama, Do Social Rights Affect Social Outcomes? (2013) (unpublished manuscript, available at ftp://ftp.econ.au.dk/afn/wp/13/wp13_18.pdf), which finds no evidence that constitutionalization of social rights improves social outcomes.

4. James Ron et al., The Struggle for a Truly Grassroots Human Rights Movement (2013), http://www.opendemocracy.net/openglobalrights/james-ron-david-crow-shannon-golden/struggle-for-truly-grassroots-human-rights-move.

5. See Michael Tomz, Reputation and the Effect of International Law on Preferences and Beliefs, Working Paper 24 (2008), available at http://www.stanford.edu/~tomz/working/Tomz-IntlLaw-2008-02-11a.pdf, which conducts an experiment that suggests that people support trade sanctions if told that it advances international law or human rights; Adam S. Chilton, The Influence of International Human Rights Agreements on Public Opinion: An Experimental Study (unpub. m.s. 2013), which finds in an experiment that people were more likely to believe that the government should halt a policy if told that it violates a human rights treaty. These studies are valuable, but their generalizability to actual conditions is limited.

6. See, e.g., Oona A. Hathaway, Do Human Rights Treaties Make a Difference?, 111 The Yale L.J. 1935 (2002); Eric Neumayer, Do International Human Rights Treaties Improve Respect for Human Rights?, 49 J. Conflict Resol. 925 (2005); Emilie M. Hafner-Burton & Kiyoteru Tsutsui, Human Rights in a Globalizing World: The Paradox of Empty Promises, 110 Am. J. Soc. 1373 (2005); Emilie M. Hafner-Burton & Kiyoteru Tsutsui, Justice Lost! The Failure of International Human Rights Law To Matter Where Needed Most, 44 J. Peace Res. 407 (2007); Linda Camp Keith, The United Nations International Covenant on Civil and Political Rights: Does It Make a Difference in Human Rights Behavior?, 36 J. of Peace Res. (1999); Daniel W. Hill Jr., Estimating the Effects of Human Rights Treaties on State Behavior, 72 J. Pol. 1161 (2010); James R. Hollyer & B. Peter Rosendorff, Do Human Rights Agreements Prolong the Tenure of Autocratic Ratifiers?, 44 NYU J.L. & Int'l Pol. 791 (2012). A mixed picture is provided in Yonatan Lupu, Best Evidence: The Role of Information in Domestic Judicial Enforcement of International Human Rights Agreements, 67 Int'l Org. 469 (2013), which finds that certain rights that are enforceable by domestic courts improve outcomes; and Yonatan Lupu, The Informative Power of Treaty Commitment: Using the Spatial Model to Address Selection Effects, 57 Am. J. Pol. Sci. 912 (2013), which finds that CEDAW improves outcomes but the ICCPR and CAT do not.

7. Yonatan Lupu, The Informative Power of Treaty Commitment: Using the Spatial Model to Address Selection Effects, 57 Am. J. Pol. Sci. 912 (2013).

8. The studies have numerous methodological difficulties; see Eric A. Posner, Some Skeptical Comments on Beth Simmons's Mobilizing for Human Rights, 44 NYU J. Int'l L. & Pol. 819 (2012); Adam Chilton & Dustin Tingley, Why the Study of International Law Needs Experiments, 52 Colum. J. Trans. L. 176 (2013).

CHAPTER FIVE

1. Kiobel v. Royal Dutch Petroleum Co., 133 S. Ct. 1659 (2013).
2. Government of the Republic of South Africa & Others v. Grootboom, Case No. CCT 11/00 (Oct. 4, 2000).

3. Id. at 944-45.

4. See Committee on Economic, Social and Cultural Rights, General Comment 3, The nature of States parties' obligations (Fifth session, 1990), U.N. Doc. E/1991/23, annex III at 86 (1991).

5. Octavio Luiz Motta Ferraz, Harming the Poor Through Social Rights Litigation: Lessons from Brazil, 89 Tex. L. Rev. 1643, 1660-62 (2011).

6. Michael Ignatieff, Human Rights as Politics and Idolatry 83 (2003).

7. Handyside v. United Kingdom, 1 Eur. Ct. H.R. 737, 753-54 (1976).

8. See Laurence R. Helfer, Overlegalizing Human Rights: International Relations Theory and the Commonwealth Caribbean Backlash Against Human Rights Regimes, 102 Colum. L. Rev. 1832 (2002).

9. Wojciech Kopczuk et al., The Limitations of Decentralized World Redistribution: An Optimal Taxation Approach, 49 Eur. Econ. Rev. 1051, 1075 (2005).

10. 554 *U.S.* 570 (2008).

11. Jeremy Waldron, Law and Disagreement (Oxford Univ. Press 2001).

12. In the United States, there was some political resistance to human rights treaties in the Senate, which has refused to consent to several of them. But in most other countries, the decision to ratify a treaty is largely in the discretion of the executive, who normally controls the government.

13. A large literature written by philosophers addresses which rights should be the subject of human rights treaties. Different philosophers propose different methods, and generate different but overlapping lists. Authors acknowledge but largely dismiss the institutional and political obstacles to implementation of their approaches, or underestimate their significance. For a sample of this writing, see James W. Nickel, How Human Rights Generate Duties to Provide and Protect, 15 Human Rights Q. 77 (1993); John Rawls, The Law of Peoples (Harvard Univ. Press 1999); Thomas Pogge, World Poverty and Human Rights (2002); Joshua Cohen, Minimalism About Human Rights: The Most We Can Hope For?, 12 J. Pol. Phil. 190 (2004); Charles R. Beitz, The Idea of Human Rights (Oxford Univ. Press 2009); Allen Buchanan, The Egalitarianism of Human Rights, 120 Ethics 710 (2010).

CHAPTER SEVEN

1. William Easterly, The White Man's Burden: Why the West's Efforts to Aid the Rest Have Done So Much Ill and So Little Good (Penguin Group 2006). The poem, though often regarded as an imperialist anthem, is not devoid of ambiguity.

2. Abhijit V. Banerjee & Esther Duflo, Poor Economics: A Radical Rethinking of the Way to Fight Global Poverty 255 (Pub. Aff. 2011).

3. Amartya Sen, Development as Freedom (Oxford, 1999).

4. Enrico Spolaore and Romain Wacziarg, How Deep Are the Roots of Economic Development?, 51 J. Econ. Lit. 325 (2013).

Further Readings

...

The literature on human rights is vast. The sources listed below played a role in my thinking but they only scratch the surface of the modern literature. A comprehensive but already dated bibliographic essay can be found in Samuel Moyn's The Last Utopia (Harvard Univ. Press 2010).

Alston, Philip, Against a World Court of Human Rights, Ethics & Int'l Aff. (forthcoming 2014).

Alston, Philip, Does the Past Matter? On the Origins of Human Rights, 126 Harv. L. Rev. 2043 (2013).

Amnesty International, Annual Report 2013, http://files.amnesty.org/air13/AmnestyInternational_AnnualReport2013_complete_en.pdf.

August, Thomas G., The Selling of the Empire: British and French Imperialist Propaganda, 1890–1940 (Greenwood Press 1985).

Banerjee, Abhijit V. & Esther Duflo, Poor Economics: A Radical Rethinking of the Way to Fight Global Poverty (Pub. Aff. 2011).

Beitz, Charles R., The Idea of Human Rights (Oxford Univ. Press 2009).

Benvenisti, Eyal, Margin of Appreciation, Consensus, and Universal Standards, 31 N.Y.U. J. Int'l L. & Pol. 843 (1999).

Buchanan, Allen, The Egalitarianism of Human Rights, 120 Ethics 710 (2010).

Caprioli, Mary & Peter F. Trumbore, Human Rights Rogues in Interstate Disputes, 1980–2011, 43 J. Peace Res. 131 (2006).

Casper, Brett A., Non-Democracies and the Exploitation of the UN Human Rights Council (August 13, 2013) (unpublished manuscript) (available at http://papers.ssrn.com/sol3/papers. cfm?abstract_id=2299762).

Chilton, Adam & Dustin Tingley, Why the Study of International Law Needs Experiments, 52 Colum. J. Trans. L. 176 (2013).

Cingranelli, David L. & David L. Richards, The Cingranelli and Richards (CIRI) Human Rights Data Project, 32 Hum. Rts. Q. 401 (2010).

CIRI Human Rights Data Project, http://www.humanrightsdata.org/ documentation.asp.

Clapham, Andrew, United Nations Charter-Based Protection of Human Rights, in International Protection of Human Rights, A Textbook 79 (C. Krause & M. Sheinin eds., Åbo Akademi Univ. 2009).

Cohen, Joshua, Minimalism About Human Rights: The Most We Can Hope For?, 12 J. Pol. Phil. 190 (2004).

Colonialism as Civilizing Mission: Cultural Ideology in British India (Harald Fischer-Tiné & Michael Mann, eds., Anthem Press 2004).

Courting Social Justice: Judicial Enforcement of Social and Economic Rights in the Developing World (Varun Gauri & Daniel M. Brinks eds. 2008).

Daalder, Ivo & James Lindsay, Democracies of the World, Unite, The American Interest (Jan./Feb. 2007), http://www.the-american-interest. com/article.cfm?piece=220.

Djankov, Simeon et al., The Curse of Aid, 13 J. Econ. Growth 169 (2008).

Donnelly, Jack, Universal Human Rights in Theory and Practice (3rd ed., Cornell Univ. Press 2013).

Drescher, Seymour, Whose Abolition? Popular Pressure and the Ending of the British Slave Trade, 143 Past & Present 136 (1994).

Dzehtsiarou, Kanstantsin & Alan Greene, Legitimacy and the Future of the European Court of Human Rights: Critical Perspectives from Academia and Practitioners, 12 German L.J. 1707 (2011).

Easterly, William, The White Man's Burden: Why the West's Efforts to Aid the Rest Have Done So Much Ill and So Little Good (Penguin Group 2006).

Edwards, Martin S. et al., Sins of Commission? Understanding Membership Patterns on the United Nations Human Rights Commission, 61 Pol. Sci. Q. 390 (2008).

Egan, Suzanne, The United Nations Human Rights Treaty System: Law and Procedure (2011).

Ferraz, Octavio Luiz Motta, Harming the Poor Through Social Rights Litigation: Lessons from Brazil, 89 Tex. L. Rev. 1643 (2011).

Ferreira, G. M. and M. P. Ferreira-Snyman, The Impact of Treaty Reservations on the Establishment of an International Human Rights Regime, 38 Comp. & Int'l L.J. S. Afr., 148 (2005).

Freedom House, Freedom in the World Country Ratings, http://www.freedomhouse.org/sites/default/files/Country%20Status%20%26%20Ratings%20Overview%2C%201973-2013.pdf.

Fukuda-Parr, Sakiko et al., An Index of Economic and Social Rights Fulfillment: Concept and Methodology, 8 J. Human Rights 195 (2009).

Fundamental Rights in Europe: The European Convention on Human Rights and Its Member States, 1950-2000 (Robert Blackburn & Jörg Polakiewicz eds., Oxford Univ. Press 2001).

Glendon, Mary Ann, A World Made New: Eleanor Roosevelt and the Universal Declaration of Human Rights (Random House 2001).

Glendon, Mary Ann, Rights Talk: The Impoverishment of Political Discourse (1993).

Goodman, Ryan & Derek Jinks, Socializing States: Promoting Human Rights Through International Law (Oxford Univ. Press 2013).

Grewal, Sharanbir & Erik Voeten, The Politics of Implementing European Court of Human Rights Judgments (Jan. 19,

2012) (unpublished manuscript) (available at http://ssrn.com/abstract=1988258).

Griffin, James, On Human Rights (Oxford Univ. Press 2008).

Hafner-Burton, Emilie M. & Kiyoteru Tsutsui, Human Rights in a Globalizing World: The Paradox of Empty Promises, 110 Am. J. Soc. 1373 (2005).

Hafner-Burton, Emilie M. & Kiyoteru Tsutsui, Justice Lost! The Failure of International Human Rights Law to Matter Where Needed Most, 44 J. Peace Res. 407 (2007).

Hafner-Burton, Emilie M., Making Human Rights a Reality (Princeton Univ. Press 2013).

Hathaway, Oona A., Do Human Rights Treaties Make a Difference?, 111 Yale L.J. 1935 (2002).

Hathaway, Oona A., Why Do Countries Commit to Human Rights Treaties? 51 J. Conflict Resol. 588 (2007).

Helfer, Laurence R., Overlegalizing Human Rights: International Relations Theory and the Commonwealth Caribbean Backlash Against Human Rights Regimes, 102 Colum. L. Rev. 1832 (2002).

Hill, Daniel W., Jr., Estimating the Effects of Human Rights Treaties on State Behavior, 72 J. Pol. 1161 (2010).

Hollyer, James R. & B. Peter Rosendorff, Do Human Rights Agreements Prolong the Tenure of Autocratic Ratifiers?, 44 NYU J.L. & Int'l Pol. 791 (2012).

Holmes, Stephen & Cass R. Sunstein, The Cost of Rights: Why Liberty Depends on Taxes (W. W. Norton 1999).

Human Rights, State Compliance, and Social Change: Assessing National Human Rights Institutions (Ryan Goodman & Thomas Pegram eds., Cambridge Univ. Press 2012).

Human Rights Watch, World Report 2013, http://www.hrw.org/world-report/2013/country-chapters.

Hunt, Lynn A., Inventing Human Rights: A History (W. W. Norton & Co. 2007).

Ignatieff, Michael, Human Rights as Politics and Idolatry (Princeton Univ. Press 2003).

Ishay, Micheline R., The History of Human Rights: From Ancient Times to the Globalization Era (Univ. of Cal. Press 2008).

Keith, Linda Camp, The United Nations International Covenant on Civil and Political Rights: Does It Make a Difference in Human Rights Behavior?, 36 J. of Peace Res. 95 (1999).

Lazarus, Liora, The Right to Security—Securing Rights or Stabilizing Rights, in Examining Critical Perspectives on Human Rights (R. Dickinson et al., eds., Cambridge Univ. Press 2012).

Lebovic, James H. & Erik Voeten, The Cost of Shame: International Organizations and Foreign Aid in the Punishing of Human Rights Violators, 46 J. Peace Res. 79 (2009).

Lebovic, James H. & Erik Voeten, The Politics of Shame: The Condemnation of Country Human Rights Practices in the UNCHR, 50 Int'l Stud. Q. 861 (2006).

Lupu, Yonatan, Best Evidence: The Role of Information in Domestic Judicial Enforcement of International Human Rights Agreements, 67 Int'l Org. 469 (2013).

Lupu, Yonatan, The Informative Power of Treaty Commitment: Using the Spatial Model to Address Selection Effects, Am. J. Pol. Sci. 57 (2013).

Kennedy, David, The Dark Sides of Virtue: Reassessing International Humanitarianism (Princeton Univ. Press 2004).

Koskenniemi, Martti, The Politics of International Law (Hart Publishing 2011).

Martinez, Jenny S., The Slave Trade and the Origins of International Human Rights Law (Oxford Univ. Press 2012).

Mearsheimer, John, The False Promise of International Institutions, 19 Int'l Sec. 5 (1995).

Meron, Theodor, On a Hierarchy of International Human Rights, 80 Am. J. Int'l. L. 1 (1986).

Moravcsik, Andrew, The Origins of Human Rights Regimes: Democratic Delegation in Postwar Europe, 54 Int'l Org. 217 (2000).

Mowbray, A. R., The Development of Positive Obligations under the European Convention on Human Rights by the European Court of Human Rights (Hart Publishing, 2004).

Moyn, Samuel, The Last Utopia: Human Rights in History (Harv. Univ. Press 2010).

Neumayer, Eric, Do International Human Rights Treaties Improve Respect for Human Rights?, 49 J. Conflict Resol. 925 (2005).

Neumayer, Eric, Qualified Ratification: Explaining Reservations to International Human Rights Treaties, 36 J. Legal Stud. 397 (2007).

Nielsen, Richard & Beth A. Simmons, Rewards for Ratification: Payoffs for Participating in the International Human Rights Regime? (2013) (unpublished manuscript, available at http://www.mit.edu/~rnielsen/ Rewards%20for%20Ratification_8oct2013_identifying.pdf).

Nussbaum, Martha C., Women and Human Development: The Capabilities Approach (Cambridge Univ. Press 2000).

Owen, John M., How Liberalism Produces Democratic Peace, 19 Int'l Sec. 87 (1994).

Peters, Anne, Humanity as the A and Ω of Sovereignty, 20 Eur. J. Int'l L. 513 (2009).

Poe, Steven C. et al., How Are These Pictures Different? A Quantitative Comparison of the U.S. State Department and Amnesty International Human Rights Reports, 1976–1995, 23 Hum. Rts. Q. 650 (2001).

Pogge, Thomas, World Poverty and Human Rights: Cosmopolitan Responsibilities and Reforms (Polity 2002).

Posner, Eric A. & David Weisbach, Climate Change Justice (Princeton Univ. Press 2010).

Posner, Eric A., Human Welfare, Not Human Rights, 108 Colum. L. Rev. 1758 (2008).

Posner, Eric A., Some Skeptical Comments on Beth Simmons's Mobilizing for Human Rights, 44 NYU J. Int'l L. & Pol. 819 (2012).

Raz, Joseph, Human Rights in the Emerging World Order, 1 Transnat'l Leg. Theory 31 (2010).

Raz, Joseph, Human Rights Without Foundations 321, in The Philosophy of International Law (Samantha Besson & John Tasioulas eds., Oxford Univ. Press 2010).

Risse, Mathias, On Global Justice (Princeton Univ. Press 2012).

Risse, Thomas & Kathryn Sikkink, The Socialization of International Human Rights Norms into Domestic Practices: Introduction, in The Power of Human Rights: International Norms and Domestic Change 1 (Thomas Risse et al. eds., Cambridge Univ. Press 1999).

Roth, Kenneth, Defending Economic, Social and Cultural Rights: Practical Issues Faced by an International Human Rights Organizations, 26 Hum. Rts. Q. 63 (2004).

Russett, Bruce & John Oneal, Triangulating Peace: Democracy, Interdependence, and International Organizations (2001).

Sen, Amartya, Development as Freedom (Knopf 1999).

Shany, Yuval, The Effectiveness of the Human Rights Committee and the Treaty Body Reform, 20 (Hebrew Univ. Fac. of Law, Int'l Law F., Research Paper No. 02-13, 2013).

Shany, Yuval, Toward a General Margin of Appreciation Doctrine in International Law?, 16 Eur. J. Int'l L. 907 (2005).

Shue, Henry, Basic Rights: Subsistence, Affluence, and U.S. Foreign Policy (Princeton Univ. Press 1996).

Simmons, Beth, Mobilizing for Human Rights: International Law in Domestic Politics (Cambridge Univ. Press 2009).

Tasioulas, John, Taking Rights out of Human Rights, 120 Ethics 647 (2010).

Vermeule, Adrian, Judging Under Uncertainty: An Institutional Theory of Legal Interpretation (Harv. Univ. Press 2006).

Versteeg, Mila & Emily Zackin, American Constitutional Exceptionalism Revisited, unpub. m.s. 2013.

Voeten, Erik, The Impartiality of International Judges: Evidence from the European Court of Human Rights, 102 Amer. Pol. Sci. Rev. 417 (2008).

Voeten, Erik, The Politics of International Judicial
Appointments: Evidence from the European Court of Human Rights,
61 Int'l Org. 669 (2007).

Vreeland, James Raymond, Political Institutions and Human Rights: Why
Dictatorships Enter into the United Nations Convention Against
Torture, 62 Int'l Org. 65 (2008).

Waldron, Jeremy, Law and Disagreement (Oxford Univ. Press 2001).

Index

...